Unusual
Prophecies
Being Fulfilled

PROPHETIC SERIES | BOOK THREE

Unusual Prophecies Being Fulfilled

DISCERNING THE FUTURE DESTINY OF AMERICA

Discovering America's Past Prophetic Patterns *and* Final Prophetic Destiny *in the* Last Days

Perry Stone

All Scripture is taken from the New King James Version of the Bible, unless otherwise indicated.

ISBN: 0-9708611-7-6
LOC: 2006900277
Copyright 2006 by Voice of Evangelism, Inc.

Voice of Evangelism Outreach Ministries
P.O. Box 3595
Cleveland, Tennessee, 37320
(423) 478-3456
Fax: 423-478-1392
www.Perrystone.org

Printed in the United States of America
Modern Way Printing & Fulfillment
8817 Production Lane
Ooltewah, Tennessee 37363

Contents

Introduction

The question is seldom asked by people of other nations, but America's spiritually hungry Christians do because they have an unquenchable thirst for knowledge and a curiosity for the mysteries of God. The question? *Is America found anywhere in Bible Prophecy?* This is not a selfish, self-serving quest to enhance our spiritual egos, it is a legitimate question. The facts are:

- ~ America is the greatest Gentile nation on the face of the earth.
- ~ America has more prosperity per capita than any Gentile nation on earth.
- ~ America has the greatest military on the planet.
- ~ America is the leading nation to promote the gospel to the world.
- ~ America is a leader in technology.
- ~ Americans read their Bibles more than the people of any nation on earth.
- ~ Americans believe in end-time prophecy more than any other Gentile nation.
- ~ America was founded as a Christian nation.

Can this nation, the strongest and the most generous to assist the poor and needy, be found anywhere in the 66 books, 1,189 chapters and 783,137 words of the Holy Bible? For centuries scholars, ministers and students of prophecy have searched, researched, and at times stretched the meanings of prophetic passages in order to pull a nugget from the text and identify America as a nation mentioned in prophecy.

After a quarter of a century of full-time ministry, I believe America's prophetic destiny will not be found in a single verse or a single chapter of the Bible, but it is to be found in the symbolism and patterns of two leading nations, past and present. Our spiritual pattern is hidden within the pattern of ancient Israel, and our political and governmental pattern is found within the patterns of the ancient Roman Empire.

This book will explore and examine these patterns, and correlate these amazing pictures with America. You will see that God may not have placed America in the systematic theology of the Word, but He has carefully hidden America within the historical context of previous ancient empires.

As you will discover, the patterns, cycles and symbolisms of these past empires parallel the developing movements and history within the United States. This is important because as the patterns progressively develop into the future, it means that the same Divine chastisements that fell on these empires will also be the destiny of America—if we continue to ignore and resist His Covenant.

This book is number three in our series, *Unusual Prophecies Being Fulfilled.* It is my personal favorite thus far.

A Servant of Christ

Perry Stone, Jr.

1

America in Prophecy: The Theories

Near the close of the first century A.D., an unknown Palestinian Jew penned a story concerning an alleged vision. He said it was revealed to him by an angel named Uriel, whom the Jews believe to be one of seven primary archangels. The vision consisted of seven revelations, one of which included a strange vision of a giant eagle. The visionary began by saying:

> On the second night I had a dream, and behold, there came up from the sea an eagle with 12 feathered wings and three heads. And I looked, and behold, he spread his wings over all the earth, and all the winds of heaven blew upon him, and the clouds were gathered about him. . . . And I looked and behold, the eagle flew with his wings, to reign over the earth and over all who dwell in it.

As the visionary continued, he revealed more detail about the eagle. From the midst of the eagle's body a voice began to speak. One wing began to reign, followed by another, then still another. The writer states, "Some of them that ruled disappeared suddenly; others rose up but did not hold the rule." The writer continues in almost a rambling fashion to describe the wings and the heads. He later writes that the eagle is one of the four beasts, alluded to in the prophecy in Daniel 7. The writer then identified the eagle as the Roman Empire.

There are some unusual correlations with the political history of America and this vision of the eagle. For example,

Two wings . . . set themselves up to reign, and their reign was brief and full of tumult.

This picture depicts the times when Lincoln and Kennedy were President in America. During both of these times the nation was struggling for civil rights, and the country was divided and filled with anxiety and fear. Another statement sounds eerily like the Civil War:

In the midst of the time of that kingdom, great struggles shall arise and it shall be in danger of falling; nevertheless it shall not fall then, but shall reign in its former power.

Some could picture Kennedy's and Lincoln's death in this:

Eight kings shall arise in it, whose times shall be short and their years swift; and two of them shall perish when the middle of its time draws near. . . .

Lincoln and Kennedy were both assassinated in the middle of their terms as presidents. The writer says that 12 feathers ruled. The 12 feathers could allude to the fact that 12 of America's presidents have served as generals in the military.

It is noted that the eagle has a left and a right wing. America has two main political parties divided between the "left wing" (Democrat) and "right wing" (Republican). The three heads of the eagle mentioned in the vision could, by a stretch of the imagination, represent the three branches of government—the judicial, executive and the legislative branches.

The entire vision is found in the book of 2 Esdras 11 and 12, and is a part of the Apocrypha. The Apocrypha is not considered inspired scripture, although it was translated from Greek to Latin and placed in the appendix of the New Testament by the Council of Trent in the 16th century. It was also added as a part of the original 1611 King James translation of the Bible, but was later removed.

Attempting to Find America in Prophecy

I call your attention to this story not as a revelation of prophecy, but to show how people attempt to discover America in prophecy. Having read the story many times, I can find various possible parallels by pulling out a verse here or there. The main point of interest is that the alleged vision exposes the prophetic future of a nation whose emblem is an eagle. America's emblem is the eagle; but the eagle was also the emblem of the Roman Empire. During New Testament times, soldiers of the Roman empire would carry large poles, called standards, with brass eagles attached to the tops of them.

No doubt America was founded and developed under the inspiration of the Almighty. From the time Columbus set sail to discover a new trade route to India and ended up 71 days later on islands off the coast of Florida, God was at work in preparing a beautiful nation. It was covered with trees, rolling hills and rugged mountains, plains and prairies, fields and forests, rivers and streams. This country was to be inhabited by a melting pot of people, all under God. The nation itself would be known as it developed and matured. Is this divine purpose revealed in the Holy Bible?

While the vision of the eagle in 2 Esdras may contain certain parallels to the United States, Bible-believing Christians must turn their attention to the inspired Holy Scriptures for an answer to the following question: Since America is the youngest of nations, is it possible we are not alluded to directly but rather indirectly, in Scripture?

Since God hides His revelations in patterns, types and shadows, perhaps we should search out possible prophetic patterns that could relate to our nation.

Ministers and scholars alike have pored over the Scriptures since the founding of the nation, hoping to find an obscure, yet clear, reference to America. Several theories have developed. Isaiah is a reference that some see as a possibility. This chapter opens by saying:

> *Woe to the land shadowed with buzzing wings, which is beyond the rivers of Ethiopia, which sends ambassadors by sea, even in vessels of reed on the waters, saying, " Go, swift messengers, to a nation tall and smooth of skin, to a people terrible from their beginning onward, a nation powerful and treading down, whose land the rivers divide." All inhabitants of the world and dwellers on the earth: When he lifts up a banner on the mountains, you see it; and when he blows a trumpet, you hear it* (Isaiah 18:1-3).

Some contend that *the land beyond the rivers of Ethiopia* in Isaiah is an allusion to America. The nation in Isaiah's vision was a land "shadowed with buzzing wings." The prophesied nation "sends ambassadors by sea." Certainly America, along with many other nations, sends ambassadors who travel across the oceans to other nations.

The nation Isaiah saw was "tall and smooth of skin." The Hebrew words mean that Isaiah saw a people who were "smooth-skinned and brightly complected." Those in northern Africa are dark complected, therefore this nation must be beyond the area of Africa—as the prophet wrote, "beyond . . . Ethiopia."

Isaiah explained that this nation is "powerful and treading down." A literal translation would be "mighty and conquering." Other Bible translations read:

~ A people dreaded near and far, that conquers and treads down (*Berkeley* translation)

~ A terror far and near; a sturdy race of conquerors (*Moffett* translation)

~ Terrible from the beginning onwards, a nation mighty (*Rotherham* translation)

Since this nation is located "beyond Ethiopia" and is well watered by rivers, it is uncertain which nation the prophet was referring to in his day. If one continues to read, however, a prophetic warning is given to this nation in verse 7:

In that time a present will be brought to the Lord of hosts from a people tall and smooth of skin, and from a people terrible from their beginning onward, a nation powerful and treading down, whose land the rivers divide—to the place of the name of the Lord of hosts, to Mount Zion.

After examining this entire passage, modern Bible interpreters are still uncertain of whom Isaiah was speaking in this prophecy. It would be useless to spend time trying to prove this reference is to America. Any attempt to "prove" this is America would simply be speculation. But there are other theories presented from Scripture.

America . . . and Jeremiah's Babylon Theory

Others, including some noted prophecy teachers, believe that Jeremiah 50 and 51 are "cryptic" references to America. When one carefully examines the text, it is clear this prophecy is *not* about America. The Hebrew prophet tells us the prophecy is against "Babylon." Since some Bible teachers compare the sins of America to those of ancient Babylon, it is easy to teach that Jeremiah's Babylonian prophecy concerns America.

The law of proper interpretation forbids reading into the text something that is not there; however, look at the words of Jeremiah. The prophet opens both chapters by saying that the prophecy is "against Babylon" (50:1, 51:1).

> ~ He says that Babylon had been a golden cup in the Lord's hand (51:7).
> ~ He notes that Babylon has fallen suddenly (v. 8).
> ~ He prophesies that "Babylon shall become heaps, a dwelling place for dragons" (v. 37).
> ~ Speaking the words of God, he warned, "My people, go out of the midst of her" (v. 45)!

It must be remembered that Jeremiah warned about Israel's 70 years of captivity in Babylon (Jeremiah 25:11). In fact, the prophet gave many firm warnings about Babylon throughout his book. So if we make the Babylon to be America in chapters 50 and 51, then we must also make the other references in Jeremiah fit America. This is literally impossible!

In fact, Jeremiah's prophecy is connected to the warnings the apostle John gave concerning "Mystery Babylon," in Revelation 17 and 18.

1. Jeremiah, speaking of Babylon, said the "rivers would dry up" (Jeremiah 50:38). In Revelation 16:12, John reveals that the Euphrates River will dry up. Ancient Babylon was built on the edge of the Euphrates River.

2. Jeremiah commanded, "Flee from the midst of Babylon" (Jeremiah 51:6). John wrote concerning Mystery Babylon, "Come out of her, my people" (Revelation 18:4).

3. In Jeremiah's vision, Babylon was a "golden cup" (Jeremiah 51:7). John repeats the same statement concerning Mystery Babylon: she has a "golden cup" in her hand (Revelation 17:4).

4. Jeremiah said "dragons" would dwell there. (Jeremiah 51:37). The Hebrew word is *tanniym* and can mean "land or sea monster." It probably alludes to some type of desert animal dwelling among the ruins. Sometimes *tanniym* is translated in the original Scriptures as "serpent" or "snake."

Several hundred years later, John said Mystery Babylon would become a habitation of devils (Revelation 18:2). It is also interesting that in Revelation 12, John described Satan as a "dragon with seven heads and ten horns" (Revelation 12:3; 9).

5. Jeremiah cried out, "Babylon is suddenly fallen" (Jeremiah 51:8). John prophesied seven hundred years later, "Babylon the great is fallen, is fallen" (Revelation 18:2).

Because the angel in Revelation 18:2 announced the fall of Babylon twice, with the phrase, "is fallen, is fallen," this could allude to two separate and distinct destructions of Babylon.

In time the Babylon of Jeremiah's day, built by King Nebuchadnezzar, fell into ruins. It was conquered by the Medes and Persians, then taken by the Greeks and Alexander the Great. Alexander was planning to restore the city to its grandeur but he died in Babylon, unexpectedly, at age 33.

After Alexander's death Babylon became the capital of the Seleucid Dynasty. The temples were eventually removed from the ancient city and a new capital was build at the Tigris River. Babylon became a ghost town but was never destroyed in the manner Jeremiah predicts—with a "destroying wind." In Revelation, John's Mystery Babylon is destroyed with fire in one hour (Revelation 18:8, 10).

It seems, therefore, that Jeremiah is predicting the fall of the Babylon in his day while projecting into the future when a "Babylon" will be burned and never inhabited again. Since John's vision in Revelation has the same phrases as Jeremiah's, then the Old Testament prophet may be alluding to a future Babylon as well as the city in his day. The author believes this could be a "dual prophecy." That is, it is a prophecy against the Babylon of Jeremiah's day when the Jews were in captivity, and a prophecy concerning Babylon that John saw in Revelation, a Babylon that would arise in the future.

It is impossible to rightly divide the Word of God and follow the basic law of Biblical interpretation by teaching that America somehow fits into the prophecy of Jeremiah. Some point out that the wickedness in America's major cities fits the pattern of Babylon. I would point out there are cities in the world much more immoral than any in America!

For example, in Western Europe, prostitution is legal in Amsterdam, Holland, and hard drugs are provided to the citizens by their government. Besides, Babylon was infamous for its idolatry and false religions, not for its immorality.

Is America the "Mystery Babylon" of Revelation 17?

The most frequent prophetic teaching people use when attempting to mark America in prophecy is the theory that America is alluded to in the prophecy of Mystery Babylon in Revelation 17. Yet again, if a person carefully examines the text, and lays "line upon line and precept upon precept," the Babylon of Revelation could not allude to America. Notice the following verses:

Then one of the seven angels who had the seven bowls came and talked with me, saying to me, "Come, I will show you the judgment of the great harlot who sits on many waters, with whom the kings of the earth committed fornication, and the inhabitants of the earth were made drunk with the wine of her fornication."

So he carried me away in the Spirit into the wilderness. And I saw a woman sitting on a scarlet beast which was full of names of blasphemy, having seven heads and ten horns. The woman was arrayed in purple and scarlet, and adorned with gold and precious stones and pearls, having in her hand a golden cup full of abominations and the filthiness of her fornication. And on her forehead a name was written:

MYSTERY, BABYLON THE GREAT, THE MOTHER OF
HARLOTS AND OF THE ABOMINATIONS OF THE EARTH.

*I saw the woman, drunk with the blood of the saints
and with the blood of the martyrs of Jesus. And
when I saw her, I marveled with great amazement*
(Revelation 17:1-6).

The imagery begins with John observing a prostitute being
carried on a beast. In the Bible, a harlot or prostitute signifies
unfaithfulness to God, or it can allude to a false religion. Some
who believe this alludes to America stretch their "prophetic
imaginations" to make the Statue of Liberty the woman on the
beast. The woman in Revelation has a golden cup, but Lady
Liberty has a torch. The statue of liberty is standing, and the
harlot of Revelation is riding. Ten kings are aligned with the
harlot, while America is controlled by an elected form of
government.

In John's prophecy, the woman was responsible for killing
the saints and was guilty of blood of the martyrs of Jesus.
America did not exist at the time of Christ's crucifixion, and
America as a nation has protected religious freedom. In John's
day the Roman Empire was guilty of crucifying Christ and
murdering thousands of early church Christians. We could
continue on, but Revelation 17:18 gives us the ultimate clue
to the identity of this woman riding the beast:

*And the woman whom you saw is that great city
which reigns over the kings of the earth* (Revelation
17:18).

The city reigning over the earth in John's day was Rome,
Italy, the heart of the Roman Empire. After the decline of Rome,
the Roman church continued to set up kings in Europe, and
literally controlled the politics of Europe and parts of the Middle

East. History indicates that thousands of Christians who refused to follow the Roman church system were persecuted and executed for their resistance. Therefore, Rome was "drunken with the blood of the martyrs."

In John's time it was common for apocalyptic writers to hide their prophecies against Rome by calling Rome, Babylon. Both Babylon and Rome invaded Jerusalem. Both destroyed the Temple and both took Jews captive as slaves. The destruction of the Jewish Temple in Jerusalem occurred on the 9th of Av, at the time of the Babylon and Roman invasions!

To say that America is the nation mentioned by Jeremiah or John would be like calling a haystack a pile of wood shavings because they both look alike from a distance. A close comparison reveals that Jeremiah's Babylon was the city located in what is now Iraq, and John's Babylon was the city of Rome, Italy. Jewish writings from the first and second centuries cryptically allude to Rome as *Babylon*, to keep Jewish writers from being persecuted by the Romans for predicting God's judgment against them.

Daniel's Empires
The More Plausible Prophecy

A theory that seems more plausible is found in Daniel 7:1-7. It is a vision the Hebrew prophet, Daniel, received while a captive in ancient Babylon. Using the symbolism of animals, the vision reveals several empires that would dominate in the future. Some have concluded that one small passage could allude to the United States.

> *In the first year of Belshazzar king of Babylon, Daniel had a dream and visions of his head while on his*

bed. Then he wrote down the dream, telling the main facts. Daniel spoke, saying, "I saw in my vision by night, and behold, the four winds of heaven were stirring up the Great Sea. And four great beasts came up from the sea, each different from the other. The first was like a lion, and had eagle's wings. I watched till its wings were plucked off; and it was lifted up from the earth and made to stand on two feet like a man, and a man's heart was given to it.

"And suddenly another beast, a second, like a bear. It was raised up on one side, and had three ribs in its mouth between its teeth. And they said thus to it: 'Arise, devour much flesh!' After this I looked, and there was another, like a leopard, which had on its back four wings of a bird. The beast also had four heads, and dominion was given to it.

"After this I saw in the night visions, and behold, a fourth beast, dreadful and terrible, exceedingly strong. It had huge iron teeth; it was devouring, breaking in pieces, and trampling the residue with its feet. It was different from all the beasts that were before it, and it had ten horns" (Daniel 7:1-7).

Notice that these "beasts" were to rule in succession. The lion was to be followed by the bear, who was followed by the leopard, who in turn was followed by the non-descriptive beast with 10 horns. Traditionally, scholars have pointed to Daniel 2 and 8 to demonstrate that the four successive empires in Daniel's prophecy are Babylon, Media-Persia, Greece and Rome.

By this interpretation, the Lion represents ancient Babylon, followed by the bear representing Media-Persia, followed by the leopard representing Greece, and the fourth beast that succeeded Greece was the Roman Empire. This premise gives distinct clarity when we are seeking to understand why Daniel saw the various animals representing various kingdoms.

The entrances of Babylon were guarded by large, stone, winged lions. Massive bears roamed the mountains in ancient Persia. The swiftness of the leopard signifies the incredible conquering ability of Alexander the Great, the head of the Grecian empire. In Daniel's vision the leopard had four wings on its back. When Alexander the Great died, his kingdom was divided between his four generals.

The final beast, with its iron teeth, can represent the iron kingdom of Rome. This is clear from the dream of Nebuchadnezzar that is recorded in Daniel 2. The "legs of iron" on the image, scholars point out, clearly represented the Roman Empire.

Yet, there is another "non-traditional" interpretation relating to Daniel's four beasts.

In the text the angel gives the meaning of the beasts, saying that "four kings will arise" (Daniel 7:17). He uses the future tense. Daniel 7 was written during Daniel's captivity in Babylon. If Babylon is listed as the first beast (the lion) and the four beasts in chapter seven "shall arise" (future tense) then perhaps the prophet was alluding to a series of end-time empires, that would rule in the latter days.

Four Modern Empires of Prophecy

Some scholars teach that these four beasts could represent four modern empires that have risen to world dominance in the past 300 years.

1. The lion represents Great Britain, whose "wings" formed the United States.

2. The bear represents the bear of Russia.

3. The leopard represents the nation of Germany.

4. The final beast represents the final kingdom that will rule at the time of the end.

First, consider Great Britain, or England, whose emblem is a lion. The British Empire was once the mightiest empire in the world. It was said the "sun never sets upon the British Empire." Britain colonized much of the world, including Palestine (present-day Israel). Notice that the lion had eagle's wings, and the wings were "plucked" or removed. The lion suddenly stood up and was given a heart like a man.

While traditional scholars indicate this alludes to Nebuchadnezzar's seven-year nervous breakdown and his recovery, as recorded in Daniel 4, others believe this speaks of how America was plucked away from the lion of Britain and England and made to stand alone. America came out of the lion and was given the heart of a man, or a heart of compassion.

The Eagle's Wings

An interesting story in early American history may indicate that Daniel 7 played a role in the selection of America's national emblem, the eagle. A Jewish man named Hayam Solomon was a broker who helped finance the American Revolution.

In my personal stamp collection, I have a U.S. postal stamp with the heading, "Contributions to the Cause," with the name Hayam Solomon, financial hero. On the back it reads:

FINANCIAL HERO

Businessman and broker Hayam Solomon was responsible for raising most of the money to help finance the American Revolution, and later to save the new nation from collapse.

After the signing of the Declaration of Independence, a committee was formed to design the seal of the United States. According to *The Federalist Brief*, Thomas Jefferson suggested a seal depicting the children of Israel being led with a pillar of cloud by day and a fire by night.

Benjamin Franklin picked up on the same theme, suggesting a seal with Moses dividing the sea and the chariots of Pharaoh being swamped under the waters. He suggested the motto: "Rebellion to tyrants is obedience to God." Again the Hebrew thread to our independence was viewed in comparison to the Hebrews coming out of Egypt. Both of these designs failed to make the final seal. A bald eagle was chosen instead.

The founder of the Institute for Judaic Christian Research believes Hayam Solomon also had input in the design for the American seal. After having studied the Book of Daniel, Solomon read where the eagle's wings were plucked from the lion. In this, he saw a prophetic picture of how America was being plucked away from the British "lion." The eagle, prophetically, would be a perfect symbol for America, he felt!

The adopted seal is printed on the back of every dollar bill. Notice that the eagle has arrows in one claw and an olive branch in the other. The arrows represent war, and the olive branch represents peace. The eagle faces the olive branch, informing us that America desires peace; but it keeps the arrows of war available as an option. Throughout America's history, she has never viewed herself as a warring nation, but has always stood ready to defend the peace if necessary. The eagle does not wear a crown as do the many coat-of-arms found in England and Britain. The crown would represent the royalty of Europe. In America's seal, the crown is omitted because the new nation would be "of the people and by the people."

Above the head of the eagle is a series of 13 stars surrounded by a circle of clouds. Today, the 13 stars are called the Megan David, or the Star of David. This same design is found on the Israeli flag and is the emblem of the modern nation of Israel.

Christians who emphasize a conspiracy theory often point to the opposite seal on the back of a dollar bill—the one with the pyramid. I have read various reports of what this "occult" seal allegedly represents. It is best to let the *Journals of Congress* reveal the meaning of the pyramid:

> Reverse. *A pyramid unfinished–of 13 layers of stone. In the zenith, an eye of Divine Providence, surrounded with a glory proper. Over the eyes these words,* "Annuit Coeptis" *(Latin words that mean "He (God) has blessed our undertakings.") On the base of the pyramid the numerical letters MDCCLXXVI.*
>
> *And underneath, the following motto,* "Novus Ordo Seclorum" *(Latin for* A New Order of the Ages*).* Source: *Our Flag and other Symbols of Americanism* by Robert Weaver, (Alexandria, Virginia, 1972), p.9.

Some call the 13 an unlucky number, but consider this:

~ There were 13 original colonies.

~ There were 13 signers of the Declaration of Independence.

~ There are 13 stripes on our flag.

~ There are 13 steps on the pyramid on the dollar bill.

~ There are 13 letters in Latin above it.

~ There are 13 letters in the motto *E Pluribus Unum*, meaning one nation from many people.

~ There are 13 stars above the eagle.

~ There are 13 bars on the shield in front of the eagle.

~ There are 13 leaves on the olive branch the eagle holds in its claw.

~ There are 13 arrows in the eagle's other claw.

Charles Thomas, Secretary of the Congress when the seal was approved, said:

> *The Pyramid signifies Strength and Duration. The eye over it and the motto allude to the many single interpositions of Providence in favor of the American cause (*The Story of the Seal *(Merrimac, MA.), p.19.*

James Wilson, one of the original justices on the Supreme Court, noted that "a free government has often been compared to a pyramid. . . . It is laid on the broad basis of the people." America could very well represent the eagle's wings that were plucked from the lion. If this is so, then it was the Almighty who first plucked the eagle's wings to form a new nation that would certainly become a major end-time, Gentile world power.

Who Are the Other Three Beasts?

If the lion could represent Britain and the eagles wings, America, then what about the other three beasts—namely, the bear, the leopard and the indescribable beast? The modern nation whose emblem has been a bear is none other than Russia. Growing up, I heard men speak of the Russian Bear.

In Daniel's vision, the bear is lying on one side and has ribs in its mouth. The bear is a devourer of flesh. The Russian Revolution of 1917 brought Communism to the nation, and because of this godless doctrine, the Russian bear has clawed his way into many nations, tearing apart those who resisted. Countless millions of innocent humans have been "devoured" as a result.

The next major nation on the world scene, after the rise of Communist Russia, was Germany. Germany had hundreds of years of rich history before Communism, but the German influence was felt worldwide with the ascension of Hitler and the rise of Nazism.

In Daniel's vision, the leopard is the third beast in order. Just as Alexander the Great did centuries before, German Nazis' "Third Reich" army moved with the speed of a leopard to conquer the surrounding nations!

Continuing this theme, a final, non-descriptive beast arises after the leopard. This is the kingdom of a man called the Antichrist in Bible prophecy.

With the final beast alluding to the last world empire before the return of Christ, this adds credibility to the thought that Daniel 7 may be a dual prophecy. It alludes to the major empires of Bible prophecy, a theory espoused by the traditional scholars, but it could also be a reference to modern end-time empires. The idea that the prophecy of the eagle's wings alludes cryptically to the United States may have some merit.

Yet, there is a final theory that we believe fits America quite well, and it is the theme we shall carry throughout this book. It is the theory of the transplanted vineyard.

The Theory of "God's Vineyard"

Perhaps the most impressive theory is one that compares Isaiah 5:1-7 with Matthew 21:33-43. It says that God would take his chosen vineyard, Israel, and transplant it to another location.

> *Now let me sing to my Well-beloved a song of my Beloved regarding His vineyard:*
>
> *My Well-beloved has a vineyard on a very fruitful hill. He dug it up and cleared out its stones, and planted it with the choicest vine. He built a tower in its midst, and also made a winepress in it; so He expected it to bring forth good grapes, but it brought forth wild grapes.*
>
> *"And now, O inhabitants of Jerusalem and men of Judah, judge, please, between Me and My vineyard. What more could have been done to My vineyard that I have not done in it? Why then, when I expected it to bring forth good grapes, did it bring forth wild grapes? And now, please let Me tell you what I will do to My vineyard: I will take away its hedge, and it shall be burned; and break down its wall, and it shall be trampled down. I will lay it waste; it shall not be pruned or dug, but there shall come up briers and thorns. I will also command the clouds that they rain no rain on it."*
>
> *For the vineyard of the Lord of hosts is the house of Israel, and the men of Judah are His pleasant plant* (Isaiah 5:1-7).

Hundreds of years later, Jesus used this parable of the vineyard in Isaiah 5 to reveal additional information concerning a new vineyard God would raise up:

Hear another parable: There was a certain landowner who planted a vineyard and set a hedge around it, dug a winepress in it and built a tower. And he leased it to vinedressers and went into a far country. Now when vintage-time drew near, he sent his servants to the vinedressers, that they might receive its fruit. And the vinedressers took his servants, beat one, killed one, and stoned another. Again he sent other servants, more than the first, and they did likewise to them. Then last of all he sent his son to them, saying, "They will respect my son." But when the vinedressers saw the son, they said among themselves, "This is the heir. Come, let us kill him and seize his inheritance." So they took him and cast him out of the vineyard and killed him.

Therefore, when the owner of the vineyard comes, what will he do to those vinedressers?

They said to Him, "He will destroy those wicked men miserably, and lease his vineyard to other vinedressers who will render to him the fruits in their seasons."

Jesus said to them, "Have you never read in the Scriptures: 'The stone which the builders rejected has become the chief cornerstone. This was the Lord's doing, and it is marvelous in our eyes?' Therefore I say to you, the kingdom of God will be taken from you and given to a nation bearing the fruits of it" (Matthew 21:33-43).

The covenant God established with national Israel was broken through their unbelief and disobedience. Israel was the true vineyard of the Almighty, but the Lord predicted God would "remove the hedge" and allow the vineyard to be trampled down. This literally occurred in the year 70 A.D.

Some of the Old Testament Hebrew prophets had been rejected and slain by their own people because the tone of their rebuke was so negative against the national sins. Then Jesus "came to His own, and His own did not receive Him" (John 1:11). Christ warned His generation that "on you may come all the righteous blood shed on the earth, from the blood of righteous Abel to the blood of Zechariah . . . whom you murdered between the temple and the altar" (Matthew 23: 35).

The parable in Matthew 23 reiterates how God sent prophets to the "vineyard of Israel" and the people of Israel slew the prophets. Jesus announced that God would "transfer" His vineyard and give it to a nation that would "bring forth fruit in its season." Most scholars believe this "nation" was the same nation Moses, Hosea and other ancient prophets foresaw.

God promised that He would one day raise up for his name a nation and a people who were not His chosen people. This "nation" is the same holy nation the apostle Peter spoke of when he says, "You are a chosen generation, a royal priesthood, a holy nation . . . who once *were* not a people but *are* now the people of God" (1 Peter 2:9, 10).

This new nation is the church, the body of Christ! When the workers in the vineyard killed the "son" then the vineyard was given over to another. After Christ's rejection in Jerusalem, God raised up the Gentiles who eventually carried the gospel of Christ to the nations of the earth. Since America has been the premier nation representing Christ to the world, could America be a part of the "transplanted vineyard?" Let's explore the prophetic history of America and see if the vineyard theme can be found.

Discovering Truth Hidden in Patterns

All scholars recognize that God uses types and shadows to hide His mysteries. The Tabernacle of Moses was patterned after the heavenly Temple. The Temple of Solomon has various correlations to the eastern gate and to the guardian angel placed at the entrance of the Garden of Eden. The Passover lamb in Exodus is a perfect picture of Christ as the Lamb of God who would suffer at the Jewish Passover season. The burning of the red heifer in Numbers 19 correlates with the crucifixion of Christ.

In order to discover hidden truth, Biblical patterns and cycles often need to be studied and examined carefully, Solomon wrote "that which has been is what will be, that which is done is what will be done" (Ecclesiastes 1:9). The future is hidden in the past, and our exploring the patterns of the past will unlock the events of the future.

With this concept in mind, I believe the prophetic birth, assignment, destiny and even possible demise of America is found by examining the historical patterns of ancient Israel and the ancient Roman Empire. America's spiritual patterns are similar to ancient Israel, and our political and governmental patterns are definitely connected to the ancient Roman Empire. To see how America is linked to Israel, we begin with a prediction God gave to Moses.

American-Hebraic Connection, The Torah

God revealed to Moses that His chosen nation, Israel, would eventually turn from their faith. The prophet was warned that Israel would be brought into captivity for their sins and God would raise up another nation to carry on the spiritual assignment of Israel.

> *The Lord will bring a nation against you from afar, from the end of the earth, as swift as the eagle flies, a nation whose language you will not understand* (Deuteronomy 28:49)

> *They have provoked Me to jealousy by what is not God; they have moved Me to anger by their foolish idols. But I will provoke them to jealousy by those who are not a nation; I will move them to anger by a foolish nation* (Deuteronomy 32:21).

This judgment was first manifested about 900 years later when the Babylonians, under King Nebuchadnezzar, invaded Israel, seized the golden vessels of the Temple, burned the holy sanctuary to the ground and took large numbers of Jews back to Babylon as captives. Six centuries later, Rome, whose emblem was an eagle and whose tongue was Latin, (not Hebrew), surrounded Jerusalem, battered the walls to the ground, burned the Temple and scattered the Jews to the four winds.

The primary sin of Israel was always the same—spiritual unbelief. God rebuked the generation in the wilderness for their unbelief, and punished them by forbidding them to inherit the Promised Land (Psalms 95:8-11). Only after the unbelieving generation died in the wilderness were their children permitted to possess the Promised Land. The sin of unbelief was the reason Christ announced judgment on his own generation (Mark 6:6; 16:14). Christ blasted the doubters and critics who resisted his miracles by telling them the wicked people of Sodom and Gomorrah would have repented in their day, had they seen the miracles of His ministry.

Jesus also warned the religious leaders of His time that their ancestors had slain the prophets and that God would require accountability for the blood of the innocent from those listening to his messages. The result of shedding innocent blood was the loss of the Temple and Jerusalem.

Christ then illustrated this with a parable—the parable of the vineyard. The vineyard was a picture of national Israel. In the story, God is the owner of the vineyard. He appointed special supervisors to oversee the watering, pruning and harvesting in the vineyard. He sent choice servants who were slain out of jealousy. Finally, the owner appointed his son (he represented Jesus) over the vineyard, and the wicked men rose up and slew the son, thinking they would then own the vineyard for themselves.

The Pharisees knew Christ was alluding to their religious hypocrisy. They whitewashed and garnished the tombs of the Hebrew prophets whom their own ancestors had murdered (Matthew 23:35-37). Christ asked this religious crowd what the master should do to the workers of the vineyard who had slain his servants as well as his own son. The crowd answered:

> They said to Him, "He will destroy those wicked men miserably, and lease his vineyard to other vinedressers who will render to him the fruits in their seasons" (Matthew 21:41).

Jesus predicted in the future, that the kingdom of God (the vineyard) would be taken from them and given to another nation:

> Therefore I say to you, the kingdom of God will be taken from you and given to a nation bearing the fruits of it (Matthew 21:43).

As stated previously, many commentators believe this new "nation" is the church which was formed by Christ. Addressing the church, Peter said, "You are a chosen generation, a royal priesthood, a holy nation" (1 Peter 2:9). The true church is the called-out believers from every race and ethnic origin who have received Christ as their Savior and Lord. Their names are written in the Lamb's Book of Life.

If we look at the word *nation* in the parable, however, a different application of the word may apply. In the New Testament, three different Greek words are translated as "nation." In the parable, the Greek word nation is *ethnos,* which can allude to a multitude, to the Gentile heathens or to a nation of people. The W.E. Vines Greek dictionary comments on this word:

> *Denotes firstly a multitude or company; then a multitude of people of the same nature of genus, nation, people; it is used in the singular of Jews (Luke 7:5; 23:2) and in the plural of nations other than Israel (In Hebrew,* goyim*).*
>
> *Occasionally it is used of Gentile converts distinct from Jews* (W.E. Vines, *Expository Dictionary of New Testament Words*, p. 484).

By examining the whole of the New Testament, it is clear the Gentiles (non-Jews) were grafted into the New Covenant (Acts 10). First century believers, both Jews and Gentiles, were called the "household of faith" (Galatians 6:10). As centuries passed, the Christian church became a predominant Gentile movement, impacting Gentile nations and converting multitudes.

The church is a spiritual nation—a spiritual kingdom with a spiritual emphasis—and not a political-military entity. There is, however, a "new" nation on earth, formed by Gentiles whose founding documents are based on the Jewish Scriptures and whose Divine assignment has been to preach the message of the Kingdom since its inception. That nation has been, and is, the United States.

America was formed out of the British Empire. Even the name *British* carries a strong Hebrew theme. The two words forming *British* in Hebrew mean, "covenant husband." *Beriyth*, in Hebrew, means "covenant;" and the word *iysh*, in Hebrew, means "husband." Some researchers identify the original British people with a link to some of the tribes of Israel. This theory is called "British Israelism," and has maintained a small, yet steady, following throughout the years.

The emblem of Britain is the Lion. The emblem of America is the Eagle. During the past 100 years, America has been considered the strongest Christian nation on earth and the staunchest ally of Israel and the Jews.

While the many theories that place America in a prophetic Biblical role may have some elements of validity, I believe the more appropriate one is the theory that God raised up America to be a *vineyard nation*. Understanding this concept reveals the link between ancient Israel and modern America.

2

Israel and America, Twin Nations of Prophetic Destiny

Then said he unto them, Therefore every scribe which is instructed unto the kingdom of heaven is like unto a man that is an householder, which bringeth forth out of his treasure things new and old (Matthew 13:52).

The deeper mysteries of the kingdom of God are often hidden, veiled through spiritual symbols, patterns, cycles and prophetic correlations. This is to hide the mysteries from worldly wisdom, and reveal the mysteries to those who will search for the truth. One method God has used to hide His mysteries is the imagery of Biblical symbolism.

For example, a serpent was used to deceive Eve in the Garden of Eden (Genesis 3:1-14). Six thousand years later, Satan is still identified as the "old serpent" in Revelation 12:8-10. The characteristics of a natural serpent parallel those of the spiritual serpent, Satan. Both are subtle, crafty, and hide to prevent exposure to their enemies.

In Exodus 12, the blood of a lamb prevented the death angel from entering the homes of the Hebrews. The power of the blood of a lamb is revealed in the New Testament, not through an animal but through Christ's death, as the "lamb of God who takes away the sin of the world" (John 1:29).

The dove is first mentioned in the story of Noah's flood, bringing an olive leaf into the ark (Genesis 8:11). In the New Testament the Holy Spirit was manifested on Christ in the form of a dove (Matthew 3). The olive leaf represents peace and the Holy Spirit is called the Comforter (John 14:16). Once a symbol is established in Scripture, its meaning usually remains consistent throughout the Bible.

Patterns are also keys to understanding the mysteries of God. The earthly tabernacle of Moses was patterned after the temple in heaven. The sacred furniture in the earthly house of God was patterned after the sacred furniture in the heavenly Temple, according to Hebrews 8:5.

Sacred Furniture	The Tabernacle	Heaven's Temple
Golden candlestick	*Exodus 25*	Revelation 1:12
Golden Altar	*Exodus 39:38*	Revelation 8:3
Ark of the Covenant	*Exodus 25:10*	Revelation 11:19

The earthly houses were reflections of the heavenly. The Hebrew nation built on earth what was built in heaven. The earthly Jerusalem was a reflection of the heavenly Jerusalem. God uses patterns so that mankind can see a picture of what is invisible—the heavenly realities of the kingdom of God!

America and Israel Patterns

Scholars admit it is difficult to uncover prophetic references to America in the Scriptures. What is unusual, however, is how the patterns of ancient Israel and America correlate. Since the Almighty uses patterns to reveal His mysteries in Scripture, perhaps we can discover the prophetic destiny of America through what I call the America-Israel patterns.

If we correlate Israel's early history and the early history of America, we can see numerous parallels that are beyond a mere coincidence. The following examples illustrate this:

~ Both nations came out of another nation.

~ Israel came out of 400 years of Egyptian bondage to reclaim their Promised Land, and America came out of England to form a new nation called the United States of America.

~ Israel, under divine inspiration, journeyed by faith, trusting God to lead them. America's founders, under divine inspiration, journeyed by faith, trusting that God would lead them and bless their efforts.

~ A sea of water separated the people from their promised land, and both nations crossed the water to reach them. Israel crossed the Red Sea, leaving Egypt behind them, and our forefathers crossed the Atlantic Ocean in ships, leaving their old countries behind them.

~ Both nations possessed the land from the natives who lived among them.

~ The Israelites found it necessary to remove the primitive and heathen *tribes* from the Promised Land in order to possess it and build their communities. The early founders of America came to this continent and often removed native American *tribes* in order to possess the land and build their towns and communities.

~ Both nations had *documents* based on the Scriptures. The primary national document initiating the moral and spiritual laws of ancient Israel was the Torah, the first five books of Moses written in the wilderness. These books revealed God's moral and spiritual instructions that Israel as a nation was required to abide by in order to experience blessing from God. America's three main documents, the Declaration of Independence, the Bill of Rights, and the Constitution are all based upon the Torah, the Prophets and the four Gospels. Both nations have the inspired words of God as their foundational principles guiding law and government.

~ Both nations had the number 13 linked to their early histories. Including the tribe of Levi, Israel had a total of *13 tribes* which entered the Promised Land in the time of Joshua. These 13 tribes, called the children of Israel, made up the nation of Israel. Out of these 13 tribes came the sons and daughters that would populate the land.

~ America was founded with *13 colonies*, which were the original 13 states of the Union. These 13 produced the sons and daughters who populated the land forming the nation of America.

~ In its early beginnings, Israel did not have a king or a capital. "Everyone did what was right in his own eyes" (Judges 21:25). Many years after Joshua, Israel asked for a king and Saul was chosen as the first king of Israel. America existed as 13 colonies for many years, and a national leader, a president, was not selected until after the formation of the United States.

~ During the reign of Israel's second king, the stronghold of Jebus was seized and called the city of David after the king who seized it. It was later named Jerusalem, and from that time forward, was the undisputed capital of Israel. After America signed the founding documents, a president, George Washington, was selected, and a new capital was called Washington. Jerusalem belonged to no tribe and was an independent city; yet it was the capital of the nation. Washington D.C. belonged to no state in the union; yet it was the capital of the United States.

~ Both countries were geographically divided between the north and the south. The tribes of Israel were eventually divided between the northern and the southern kingdoms. In America, the nation experienced a major division between the north and the south at the time of the Civil War.

~ Both have had to deal with Babylon. Many years after Israel settled the land and constructed the Temple in Jerusalem, there was a major conflict with the Babylonians (the area of present-day Iraq). These invaders terrorized the Jews, burning their homes, seizing their money and destroying their holy Temple. After hundreds of years of living in security, Americans were attacked by Islamic fanatics from the same area of the Middle East where ancient Babylonians once ruled.

~ In the 9/11 attacks we saw our buildings burn, experienced a loss of jobs and entered a financial recession.

America, with the younger civilization, went to war with Iraq, the land of one of the oldest civilizations! Israel warred with Babylon long ago, and today our troops are warring in the land of ancient Babylon!

~ May 14 is a significant date for both countries. The Jews were scattered throughout the world for about 19 centuries. Finally, on May 14, 1948, the British mandate ended at midnight, and Israel was reborn as a nation, literally, in one day! May 14 is also linked to America. On May 14, 1607, we formed our first colony!

These amazing patterns indicate that God has marked America as a chosen nation, just as He did ancient Israel for His chosen people. There is no other nation on earth whose early history parallels Israel—only the United States.

Both have dealt and are dealing with Islamic terrorism. Jihadists and Islamic extremists have successfully plotted against the modern Jewish state of Israel, taking the lives of thousands of innocent Jewish people. America has also dealt with Islamic terror cells which have struck New York and Washington D.C., and continue to plan other assaults.

Correlating the Sacred Furniture

One of the most interesting features in the spiritual linking of Israel and America is found in the patterns of the Tabernacle furniture. God instructed Moses to built sacred furniture for the wilderness Tabernacle which would be used in the worship and sacrifices of the Tabernacle. There were seven major pieces of furniture listed by Moses:

~ The Brass Altar   - Exodus 27:6

~ The Brass Laver   - Exodus 30:18

~ The Gold Menorah   - Exodus 25:31

~ The Table of Shewbread   - Exodus 25:30

~ The Altar of Incense   - Exodus 30:1

~ The Veil of Separation   - Exodus 26:33

~ The Ark of the Covenant   - Exodus 25:10

The Tabernacle was a large rectangular tent, measuring approximately 208 feet long by 104 feet wide. The only entrance was through a main curtain that hung on the east side. Once a person entered the sacred compound, he discovered three distinctive areas: the Outer Court, the Inner Court and the Holy of Holies. The two pieces of furniture in the Outer Court were the brass altar and the brass laver.

One entered the Inner Court through a veil, and found three more pieces of holy furniture. To the right was the table of shewbread, to the left was the golden, seven-branched candlestick. Directly in front was the golden altar. Only the High Priest could enter the Holy of Holies, and he did it by passing through a final, heavy veil. Inside the Holy of Holies was a single piece of furniture, the Ark of the Covenant. Each piece of furniture had a particular feature or substance that distinguished it from the other pieces.

   ~ The brass altar contained *three fires* that burned continuously.

   ~ The brass laver was filled with *water*.

   ~ The table of shewbread had 12 *loaves* of bread placed on it each week.

   ~ The seven lamps on top of the Menorah were filled with *oil*.

   ~ *Incense* was burned on the golden altar every morning.

~ The lid to the Ark of the Covenant was called the
   Mercy Seat, and was covered with *gold.*

If you placed a map of the contiguous 48 states on a table
and put a box around it, it would be, roughly, a large rectangle.
While the Tabernacle had three divisions: the outer court, the
inner court and the Holy of Holies, America is divided into the
East, the Midwest and the West. Beginning in the east and
moving westward, place the sacred furniture on this map of
America. It is amazing to see how the substance, or feature, of
each piece fits a particular area on the map.

Mapping the Tabernacle

Place the *Brass Altar* on the area of Tennessee, the edge of
North Carolina and Kentucky. The three fires burning on the
brass altar correlate with these three states where the first
revival fires of the latter-day outpouring of the Holy Spirit in
North America was reported.

These three states are also the areas where some of the
early Pentecostal revivals birthed major full gospel
denominations. Thus, the three fires on the brass altar
correlate to the three states where the early fires of revival
helped initiate the full gospel movement.

The *Brass Laver* would fit in the area of the Mississippi River,
easily recognized as the main waterway in America. The
Mississippi River is used to move huge barges loaded with
millions of tons of coal, steel, food and other vital products in
America. The water in the laver correlates with the main
watercourse in America.

The *Menorah* sat on the south end of the inner court. On the
American map this would be positioned in the regions of Texas

and Oklahoma. The Menorah was replenished each day with oil to keep the lamps burning in the Tabernacle and Temple. *Both Texas and Oklahoma are known as the oil states of America.* Much of the wealth from both of these states comes from drilling for oil and natural gas. Therefore, the oil of the Menorah correlate with the products of these two states.

The pattern continues with the *Table of Shewbread.* The bread on this table came from the wheat grown in Israel. In the Tabernacle this table was in a direct line north of the Menorah. On the American map this table of bread would be positioned in the states of Kansas and Nebraska, the center of the breadbasket of America. Bread is the central feature on the table and the grain grown in Kansas and Nebraska make our bread, which is more than a coincidence.

Traveling from east to west in a direct line in the Tabernacle the next holy fixture would be the *Golden Altar of Incense.* On this map of America, the Golden Altar of the Tabernacle would be placed in the region of Colorado.

At first this is somewhat difficult to correlate—until you realize that there were 11 (some say 13) different spices used in the incense on the Golden Altar. The color of the incense was red. Hot coals from the brass altar were used to burn the incense. Colorado has numerous mines, including coal mines, and is a state with many minerals. The Colorado River is known as the Red River.

Purpose in God's Design

If the information appears to be merely coincidental thus far, then consider the following. A giant veil divided the Inner Court from the Holy of Holies. On the map, this veil would need to be placed past Denver, moving on toward the west coast of

America. A satellite photograph reveals a land split, a division, running north to south called the continental divide. This would fit the same area of the large veil in the tabernacle!

After passing through the veil, the final chamber was the Holy of Holies. It housed the Ark of the Covenant. The Ark was a wooden box, covered inside and out with pure gold. The lid was called the Mercy Seat and two gold cherubim sat on the lid, looking down at the seat of mercy.

On the map of America, the Ark of the Covenant would be placed in the states of Nevada and California. The main substance of the Ark was gold, and the state of California was formed by the famous gold rush. At the turn of the 20th century, a revival called the Azusa Street revival, began in Los Angeles and spread throughout the world. The revival featured the preaching of repentance and revealed God's *mercy* to the nation.

Are these picture parallels a strange coincidence or merely the imagination of a prophetic teacher? Or, do they reveal in picture form how God designed the United States to correlate to His revelation of the Tabernacle? If so, why would God be interested in a place such as America?

The answer may lie in the spiritual foundation of our nation. The Tabernacle and the Temple was both designed as places of redemption for the nation. They provided a meeting place between the Almighty and His people. I believe America was founded to proclaim the redemptive plan of God to the nations of the world. Hundreds of thousands of churches scattered throughout the nation minister to over 40 percent of the population.

America has become a spiritual dwelling place for the Christian faith, just as Israel was a dwelling place for the covenant people. America has become a safe haven for the

Jewish people in times of global disasters and holocausts, which brings to mind this prophecy in Isaiah:

> *And there will be a tabernacle for shade in the daytime from the heat, for a place of refuge, and for a shelter from storm and rain* (Isaiah 4:6).

This unique link connecting America to ancient Israel continues with more than just symbolism and patterns. We also see many correlations connecting this spiritual chain with the founding and early development of America, as the following chapter reveals.

3

America's Foundation:
The Judeo-Christian Link

*Who serve the copy and shadow of the heavenly
things, as Moses was divinely instructed when he
was about to make the tabernacle. For He said,
"See that you make all things according to the
pattern shown you on the mountain"* (Hebrews 8:5).

The Almighty raised up America following some of the same
spiritual patterns as He used with His chosen nation, Israel.
Our earliest history is traced to Christopher Columbus and his
famous journey to the Indies, which ended up as a journey of
prophetic destiny. Columbus was born in Italy. Some
researchers believe that his parents were actually Jewish
refugees to Spain. Columbus boasted that he was a descendent
of King David. The name, Columbus, came from the name *Colon*,
a commonly used name among Jews living in Spain.

Several interesting aspects of this man's life lend to the possibility of a strong Jewish link, either in his ethnic background or in his religious belief. In 1492, Columbus spoke of the Jewish Temple in the time of Christ as being the Second House, a term used among the Jews of his day. He also dated the destruction of the Jewish Temple in Jerusalem at 68 A.D. instead of in 70 A.D., which was a Jewish belief in his day.

As Columbus set out to make his journey, he wrote in his diary:

> *It was the Lord who put it into my mind, (I could feel His hand upon me), the fact that it would be possible to sail from here to the Indies. All who heard of my project rejected it with laughter, ridiculing me. There is no question that the inspiration was from the Holy Spirit, because He comforted me with rays of marvelous inspiration from the Holy Scriptures.*
>
> *I did not make use of intelligence, mathematics or maps. It is simply the fulfillment of what Isaiah had prophesied (from* The Diary of Christopher Columbus*).*

The ships and their crews were ready for the journey, but Columbus delayed the trip for an additional day. The scheduled day to embark was the 9th of Av on the Hebrew Calendar. This was a fast day for all Jews to commemorate the destruction of the Temple. It is considered the worst day of the year, throughout Jewish history. Columbus delayed the start of his trip. This action may have been initiated by the Jewish men on his boats.

Among the numerous Jewish men aboard were the map and chart man, Abraham Zekuto, and Joseph Vachinn, the nautical "engineer." With the Spirit of the Lord directing Columbus' voyage, he soon found his ships in the midst of the sea. After 70 days, however, he realized a mutiny was about to occur. On the 71st day, they spotted land.

That day on the Jewish calendar was the last day of the Jewish feast of Tabernacles, Hashannah Rabbah. On this day a special prayer is prayed, remembering how God directed Israel across the sea and saved them from destruction. And on this day God saved Columbus' ships, stopped the mutiny and provided the climax for the journey.

When Luis da Torres left the ship and began to speak with the natives, he spoke Hebrew and Aramaic, thinking the natives may speak Hebrew or could be linked to the lost tribes of Israel.

This possible Hebrew link continues when we examine the signature of Columbus. When writing personal and private letters to Diego Colon, his son, Columbus signed his name with a triangle. Jewish scholars note that this form of signature was known among the mystics of his day. In letters to his son, two letters appear to be in the shape of the Hebrew letters *bet* and *hei*, denoting the Hebrew blessing *b'ezrat haShem*, meaning "with the help of God."

Parallels with the Early Founders

The founding fathers and early leaders of America were aware of the spiritual significance of what they were doing and how God was directing their destiny. William Bradford, one of the first governors, wanted to make Hebrew the official language of the colonies. Because Jews were scattered throughout the world, some suggested that America should provide a section of land to which the Jews could immigrate and form a nation of Israel inside of America.

Even the early settlers considered themselves spiritual Jews who were settling a new Promised Land. The fact that so many of the rural towns in early America were given Biblical names is evidence that early settlers were very conscious of Holy Scriptures and God's Hand in their plans.

History indicates that our founders came to this continent seeking freedom of religion, not freedom from religion as some today are seeking. In 1607, about 100 Pilgrims traveled across the sea from England, eventually landing in Virginia and forming the Jamestown colony.

The colony was named after King James who authorized a translation of the Bible into the English language. The ship's carpenter and two soldiers raised a large cross in the sand, and the land was dedicated to God. The severe winter took the lives of almost the entire colony; however, 50 survived and began to settle the region.

In 1620, the famous Mayflower ship brought Pilgrims to the shores of Cape Cod. Those on the journey formed the Mayflower Compact. The document began:

> *In the name of God, Amen. We, whose names are under-written, the Loyal Subjects of our dread Sovereign Lord, King James, by the Grace of God, of England, France and Ireland, King, Defender of the Faith, etc. Having undertaken for the Glory of God, and Advancement of the Christian Faith, and the Honor of our King and Country, a voyage to plant the first colony. . . .*

Over 100 years later, 200 Lutherans migrated from Austria seeking religious freedom in Georgia. America was the land of religious freedom. Most of our founders and early fathers were religious. The majority of the population held the Christian faith.

Mary's Land and George Calvert

George Calvert was a Catholic who lived in England. His beliefs were not accepted in England, since the Church of England was the only church accepted in the nation. Seeking religious freedom, George, also known as Lord Baltimore, moved to Virginia and was not accepted by the Protestants. He eventually was given permission to go north of Virginia and settle a land he named Mary Land, after the wife of one of England's kings.

After Calvert's death, 250 Catholics traveled from England on two ships called the Ark and the Dove. They traveled up the Potomac to a place they named Saint Mary's, after the mother of Christ. There they erected a cross and dedicated the land to the Christian faith. In England, the settlers of what would become Maryland were called *redemptioners*.

In 1649, Maryland law read, "No person whatsoever within this Province professing to believe in Jesus Christ shall be in any way troubled or persecuted for his or her religion, nor in any way forced to practice another religion."

The Holy Experiment

Another man, William Penn, had the idea of conducting a "holy experiment." He said, "If I had a colony of my own, I would make it a place of true Christian and civil liberty." Penn was of the Quaker faith and wanted land from the king to settle for his holy experiment.

England's King Charles owed the Penn family a great sum of money. William asked the king to repay the family with a large piece of land in America. Penn took the land between Maryland and New York.

Penn wanted to name the territory, Sylvania, because of the lovely wooded area. The king suggested Pennsylvania, meaning Penn's woods, in honor of Penn's father Admiral Penn. William Penn wrote about this land:

> *I looked to the Lord for it, and I owe it to His hand and power. . . . I believe He will bless and make it the seed of a nation. I will be careful to set up a good government there.*

The leading city of Pennsylvania is Philadelphia, which is mentioned in the Bible (Revelation 3:7). The name comes from two words meaning *love of brothers*. Philadelphia is called the city of brotherly love. Penn's commitment to a land of peace and religious freedom prepared the way for the United States of America. Many states were founded in similar manner by men of faith who knew God's hand was on the new land.

Early Colleges Were Christian

Many of the Ivy League colleges were founded *by* Christians and *for* Christians. Dartmouth in New Hampshire was originally started by a minister, the Reverend Eleazar Wheelock, in 1769. The inspiration for the school began when Wheelock started teaching Native American Indians the Christian faith and training them to be missionaries to their own people.

Evangelist George Whitfield initiated contact with the Earl of Dartmouth when Wheelock requested support for the school. The Earl provided 10,000 pounds (approximately $18,000 today), and a charter from the king was granted. This Indian missionary school eventually became filled with white students.

In August 1768, John Witherspoon and his wife arrived at Princeton, New Jersey. Reverend Witherspoon began training young men at a college known as Princeton. He served as president of the college for 26 years, graduating over 478 students. Of these graduates, one became a U.S. President, one a Vice President, and 10 served as assistants to the President. Thirteen became state governors, three sat as U.S. Supreme Court judges, 21 were elected as U.S. senators and 39 became U.S. congressmen. I would say this preacher of the gospel had a direct impact, through his leadership, at Princeton.

The name *Charles Finney* is associated with great evangelistic crusades where thousands attended to hear the former lawyer expound the Bible. After years of engaging in a traveling ministry, Finney became tired and ill; so he settled in New York to pastor. Thousands who were converted in his ministry chose to train for Christian service, but were having difficulty finding schools that would stand against slavery or injustice.

Finney's followers went to the officials at Oberlin College in Oberlin, Ohio, with an offer: "Invite Finney to teach in this school and allow black students to attend, and we will enroll in your school." Oberlin agreed. Finney began teaching in 1835, eventually becoming the college's second president.

From its beginning Oberlin College offered blacks as well as whites a good education, and became the center of a movement to end slavery. Oberlin was also the first college in America to award bachelor's degrees to women. Finney felt there was no separation between serving God in church and in public. He encouraged Americans to vote in honest leaders as it was their duty to God. This minister made an impact through education in this college.

Even the well-known and respected universities of Yale and Harvard were once Christian colleges and were involved in training ministers for the new nation. Today, little vestige of a Christian foundation can be found in most of the early institutes of higher learning.

Preachers in Politics

Today, liberal secularists nearly have a stroke if they think a conservative Christian is becoming involved in the local or state political scene. Such civic-minded citizens are soon painted as intolerant right winged extremists. This was not true with early America.

John Peter Gabriel Muhlenberg was parson (pastor) of the Woodstock Lutheran congregation. One Sunday morning when he was preaching, he removed his clerical robe and revealed he was wearing a Continental Army uniform. Dramatically, he announced he was going to fight for America's independence!

Suddenly, the men in the congregation began rising, yelling, "We will go too!" The preacher led a Virginia regiment into battle, and after two years he was made a Brigadier General. Before the Revolution, ministers used the pulpit to preach about American independence, and encouraged the men to join the minutemen and fight for freedom.

The same is true before the Civil War. Many pulpits in the south promoted slavery and many in the north resisted it, demanding the freedom of blacks in America.

About a hundred years later another minister, Martin Luther King, Jr., organized ministers and church congregations in the south to march for the civil rights of blacks in America. Despite objections from secularists, atheists and others, America's greatness can be found in the pulpits and pews of this nation. This has been true from the earliest time to the present.

Hebraic Patterns in the Nation's Capital

The first living creature was like a lion, the second living creature like a calf, the third living creature had a face like a man, and the fourth living creature was like a flying eagle (Revelation 4:7).

John saw a vision of the heavenly Temple and the throne room. Standing at the four corners of the throne were four living creatures, with the faces of a lion, a calf, a man and an eagle. These beings are called living creatures and participate in the worship of God, saying, "Holy, holy, holy, Lord God Almighty" (Revelation 4:8)!

When Moses established the Tabernacle in the wilderness, God instructed the 12 tribes to be divided into groups of three to the north, three to the south, three to the east and three to the west. In each of these four divisions was one main tribe. Dan was the main tribe in the north, Judah in the east, Reuben in the south and Ephraim to the west.

Each of the 12 tribes was given a special emblem that became an emblem of its tribe. Dan was pictured as an eagle, Judah was a lion, Reuben was a man and Ephraim was a bull or an ox. These four emblems are identical to the four living creatures standing before the Lord.

At our nation's capital, there is a large rectangular area called the Washington Mall. In the center of the mall is the Washington Monument, a huge obelisk sitting silently as a memorial to our first president. Four main federal buildings make up the four main areas of the mall. To the north is the White House, the home of America's president.

Directly to the east is the Capitol building where elected officials from all 50 states meet to enact legislation for the nation. To the south is the famous Jefferson memorial and to the west is the Lincoln memorial. If we look at the emblems that represent these four important buildings, a strange correlation develops.

The emblem of the U.S. president is the eagle. When the U.S. President speaks, his seal, the eagle, is placed on the front of the podium. This correlates with the tribe of Dan.

While the Capitol has no direct seal, it is the place where the laws of the land are made. In Biblical prophecy the tribe of Judah was called the "lawgiver." In Psalm 60:7, God said, "Judah is My lawgiver." And Judah's emblem was the lion.

The emblem of Reuben, a man, correlates with the symbol of Thomas Jefferson. This early founder was considered a deist, one who believes there is a supreme Being who places all control in the hands of men. Today, we would consider one who believes that all authority, control and power of nations are in the hands of men as a secular humanist. Thomas Jefferson represents a man, the emblem of Reuben.

The fourth emblem is linked to the life of Lincoln, whose memorial is on the western end of the mall. Lincoln was considered a simple man who was raised on the frontier. During his administration the Civil War tore the nation apart, dividing the north and the south. The first battle of the Civil War took place in Manassas, Virginia, and the tribe of Manasseh was camped in the west in ancient times. The ox, or the bull, was the emblem of Manasseh, and the first Battle of Manassas was called the Battle of Bull Run!

Some may suggest that this is stretching our insight to vindicate the Israel-America link, but these things correlate too closely to be mere coincidence. Remember, the Washington Monument sits in the center of the mall. Before it was constructed, some suggested that a large Temple be erected in the center of the mall.

The Kings of Israel and America's Presidents

Another interesting feature of America's Hebraic links relate to the kings of Israel and America's Presidents. According to the Biblical record, King Saul was the first king of Israel from the tribe of Benjamin. Saul ruled for 40 years.

After Saul's death, David was exalted to king and he also ruled 40 years. Following David's death, his son Solomon ruled for a period of 40 years, making a total of 120 years. Solomon's son followed his father to the throne after Solomon's death. This son, Rehoboam, was wicked; and under his rule, the 12 tribes of Israel were divided.

From this point until the Babylonian captivity, Israel was divided between the northern and southern kingdoms. Before the Babylonian invasion there were 19 kings in the north, which was called Israel; and 20 kings in the south, which was called Judah. The total kings were:

3 Monarchial Kings (Saul, David and Solomon)

19 Northern Kings

20 Southern Kings

---

42 Total Kings from Saul to the Babylonian Captivity

Prior to the invasion of Nebuchadnezzar and the destruction of Jerusalem, the king in Judah was Zedekiah. The Babylonians invaded the Holy City and seized it between the 9th and 11th years of King Zedekiah. How does this pattern correlate with the presidents of the United States?

~ America's first President was George Washington. He was a head taller than the average American, and at first he did not desire to be the President. This is similar to Israel's first King, Saul. He was a head taller than the average Israelite. At first he did not want to be the King, but was chosen from among the people (see 1 Samuel 9).

~ From Saul, the first king, to the time of war with Babylon was several hundred years. By the time of king number 42, the Babylonians had initiated an invasion on Israel soil. From George Washington to Bill Clinton, we had 42 Presidents.

~ Clinton was President for the eight years from 1992 to 2000. He was sworn in after the conclusion of a major war called the Gulf War. This war was fought in the Persian Gulf area, however, the war was a direct conflict with Saddam Hussein, President of Iraq.

~ Scholars note that Iraq is the land of ancient Babylon. Just as war between Israel and Babylon was waged during the time of the 42nd king of Israel, so Islamic terrorists from the Middle East began their assaults on America during the administration of America's 42nd President.

~ During eight years of Clinton's administration, a series of terrorist attacks were initiated against America and our interests abroad. These sudden and devastating assaults include the bombings of two U.S. embassies in Africa, the bombing of the USS *Cole* battleship and a premeditated bombing of one of the Twin Towers in New York in 1993.

~ Evidence has since mounted that terrorists were planning a major attack during the Clinton administration, between 1999 and 2000. These attacks, along with the attack of 9/11, eventually led America into a war against terrorism in Afghanistan and Iraq.

~ The invasion of Israel by Nebuchadnezzar occurred in the ninth year of Zedekiah's reign. From 1992 until the year 2001 was nine years, and 2001 was the year America was hit by terrorists in New York and Washington, D. C.

Another pattern emerges when counting the generations from Abraham to the New Covenant:

So all the generations from Abraham to David are fourteen generations, from David until the captivity in Babylon are fourteen generations, and from the captivity in Babylon until Christ are fourteen generations (Matthew 1:17).

~ According to Matthew, there were 42 total generations from the time of Abraham, father of the first covenant, to Christ, the mediator of the new covenant. Eventually, Jerusalem was destroyed again by the Roman 10th Legion, within a generation from the time of Christ.

~ Another correlation is evident when a person counts the total Biblical generations from Enoch to the captivity of Babylon, which again adds up to 42 generations. Enoch was the seventh man from Adam and was translated into heaven. The Babylon captivity came after 42 generations.

The Prophetic Number 43

George W. Bush became the 43rd President of the United States. The number 43 is interesting as it relates to the redemption of Israel. For example, Yom Kippur (the Day of

Atonement) occurred each year on the 10th day of the 7th month. During this time the High Priest would offer a bull, a ram, a goat and lambs on the altar. The blood of these animals was ritually sprinkled on the sacred furniture, including the Ark of the Covenant, the four corners of the Golden Altar and the Menorah. From the beginning to the conclusion of the service, the blood of the sacrifices was sprinkled 43 times.

> *Thus he had sprinkled* forty-three times *the expiatory blood, taking care that his own dress should never be spotted with the sin laden blood.* (Alfred Edersheim, *The Temple.* P. 316).

For some time I have stated that I believe this number, 43, speaks of fullness. The Bible indicates that the coming of the Lord is linked to three things becoming "full," the fullness of the Gentiles, the fullness of Israel, and the fullness of iniquity.

> *For I do not desire, brethren, that you should be ignorant of this mystery, lest you should be wise in your own opinion, that blindness in part has happened to Israel until the fullness of the Gentiles has come in* (Romans 11:25).

> *Jerusalem will be trampled by Gentiles until the times of the Gentiles are fulfilled* (Luke 21:24).

National Israel and many of the Jewish people's eyes have been veiled to the knowledge of Jesus as their Messiah. For centuries the traditions of the rabbis have restrained the Hebrew people from clearly examining the Scriptures to identify their Messiah and to see how Christ fulfilled the prophecies.

During this same time, Gentile nations such as Great Britain and America welcomed the teaching of the gospel and sent missionaries throughout the world to spread the light of the gospel to surrounding Gentile nations. For centuries Great

Britain and America were considered Christian nations. The first translation of the Bible into the English language that was printed and distributed to the English speaking world was the 1611 King James Version.

Since the year 2001, one would think that Americans would turn to God and begin to emphasize the importance of repenting of their national sins. Americans became patriotic, but did not repent. In fact, organizations such as the ACLU have increased the pace of lawsuits to remove the Ten Commandments, nativity scenes, crosses and the name of God off of public landmarks.

England has basically backslid as a nation, as most mainline churches are empty and over 300 have been turned into Islamic Mosques. Light among the traditional Christian Gentile nations is beginning to slowly diminish in the eyes of the people in the major population centers. The veil is slowly being lifted, however, and the light is being revealed to many souls living in the nation of Israel.

I have spoken with several Jewish evangelists from Israel who have said that since the year 2001 there has been a major increase of interest in Jews studying the Bible, researching prophecy and discovering the details of the passion of Christ.

Paul spoke of this phenomenon when he wrote of the olive tree in Romans 11. Paul said the natural tree was Israel and the wild olive tree was the Gentiles. He revealed that because of Israel's spiritual unbelief toward Christ, some of the natural branches were severed from the tree.

The wild Gentile branches were grafted in, however, and through the root of the tree, the Gentiles received strength and growth. Paul then warned that if the Gentiles turn to unbelief, God is able to graft again the Jewish branches into the tree.

Even journalists acknowledge that George Bush, the 43rd President, has been one of the most publicly religious presidents since Abraham Lincoln or George Washington. If America's prophetic cycles are significant to the prophetic meaning of Biblical numbers, then the number 43 speaks of completion or transition.

This completion could allude to the climax of America's position as the leading Gentile world power as attention moves from west to east, from America to Europe. The transition could be one of many changes to come after the 2008 cycle arrives.

America and the 2007-2008 Cycle

Since the early 1990s, I have pointed out that there is a major prophetic cycle pointing to the year 2007-2008 and beyond for America. This same cycle is found in the prophetic cycles of Israel. The first major prophetic timeframe is a period of 400 years. There are actually several time periods of 400 years in the long history of Israel. The earliest recorded 400-year cycle was when Israel went into Egypt and lived among the Egyptians for 400 years. The Lord revealed this cycle to Abraham before it happened:

> Then He said to Abram: "Know certainly that your descendants will be strangers in a land that is not theirs, and will serve them, and they will afflict them four hundred years. And also the nation whom they serve I will judge; afterward they shall come out with great possessions (Genesis 15:13, 14).

The children of Israel spent 400 years in Egypt; and at the conclusion of this time, God initiated a great deliverance and brought 600,000 men, with their families, out of Egypt to the Promised Land. America's 400-year cycle is as follows. Our first colony was formed May 14, 1607. Moving forward 400 years takes us to the year 2007. What moral and spiritual changes will we see as America enters a new cycle in its history? If our patterns fit ancient Israel, something new or different could be in store for our nation.

Another interesting pattern emerges beginning with the year 1917. This year began the conclusion of World War I. During the war a Jewish chemist named Chaim Weizman assisted the British in developing a chemical used to make explosives. His assistance was so important that after the war he was asked if there was something special that could be done for him and his family. He requested that a declaration be made giving the Jews permission to live in Palestine.

The official proclamation allowing Jews to immigrate to Palestine was revealed in a letter from British Foreign Secretary Arthur James Balfour to Lord Rothschild on November 2, 1917. This document is known as the Balfour Declaration. From 1917 to the year 2007 is a period of 90 years; Sarah was 90 years of age when Isaac was born.

Does the year 2007-2008 allude to major prophetic events related to Israel? Will God begin to focus on the Jews as the age of the Gentiles begins to come to a climax (Romans 11:25)? Time will tell.

The 40-Year Cycle

Jesus predicted that the Jerusalem Temple would be destroyed and the stones would be toppled on one another (Matthew 24:1, 2). This was fulfilled in the year A.D. 70, when the Roman 10th Legion sacked the Holy City, seizing the Temple treasures and burning the sanctuary to the ground. Jesus gave his Olivet discourse sometime around the year A.D. 30. Forty years later, the prophecy was fulfilled. Forty years of unbelief are considered a generation in Scripture (Psalm 95:10).

There appears to be a correlation between the reunification of Jerusalem and still another generation of unbelief. Israel was re-birthed as a nation in 1948; however, Jerusalem was divided between Jordan in the east and Israel in the west. A giant concrete wall separated the two divisions of the city.

During an amazing six-day war in June of 1967, the Jordanians lost control of the eastern half of the city and the Israelis annexed the eastern half into the western half, uniting Jerusalem as the capital of Israel. From 1967 to 2007 is a period of 40 years. Remember that 40 years is related to a generation of unbelief. Israel had to wander in the wilderness for 40 years because of their unbelief. Jesus called his generation a generation of unbelief.

The time frame of 2007-2008 appears to be linked to Israel and perhaps the fullness of the Gentiles. I believe, somehow, this cycle is also linked with America. We can already see hatred toward Christianity, Christian symbols and Christian celebrations, as laws are being passed to hinder or stop our Christian heritage. This unbelief, spreading like a cancer, may be prophetic. These attitudes may be the door that enables the New World Order to form the next empire of Bible prophecy.

The Importance of 2008

The year 2008 introduces the 44th President of the United States. In Biblical terms, the number 4 is an earthly number. There are *four* points of the compass, and *four* rivers flowed from the Garden of Eden. The 44th generation from Adam suffered the heat of captivity in Babylon! At that time the godly, covenant people were made subject to new laws which limited their prayer life and brought persecution. Those who did not accept other gods, but maintained that there was only one true God, suffered!

Is It Time for a Woman President?

In the 1980's senator Walter Mondale was nominated by his party to run for President of the United States. The senator broke ranks and selected Geraldine Ferraro to join his ticket as the first women vice presidential candidate. This caused quite a stir and the ticket failed, as Ronald Reagan became the new President.

During every presidential election year since that time, the discussion reappears that it may be time for America to vote in a woman president. Actually, many nations of the world have women who have either led the nation or have had very high positions in the government. The queen mother rules England. India and the Philippines have both seen women direct their nations. In America, no distinction is made between men and women in politics.

We also must acknowledge what God's Word declares, that in the last days His Spirit will be poured out among sons and daughters, servants and handmaidens (Acts 2:17, 18). It is clear that in Christ there is no gender difference (Galatians 3:28). Therefore, in the sight of the Lord there would be no difference between a man or a woman directing the nation.

The moral character of any man or woman is of utmost concern, however, when we realize that personal ideology formulates the laws and releases the same spirit over the nation.

The Seven Prophecies

From time to time very godly, praying persons will receive a clear Word from the Lord that relates to future events. In the New Testament this is called a *prophecy*. The prophetic gift is for the edification, exhortation and comfort of the believer (1 Corinthians 14:3). Through this unique gift the Holy Sprit can show the church things to come.

William Branham was the leading voice in the wave of healing revivals in the 1940s and 1950s. This revival movement gave rise to the Charismatic Movement in the late 1960s. A small, meek, middle-aged servant of Christ, Branham's life was so filled with out-of-the ordinary, supernatural encounters with God that had there been no eyewitnesses and close associates to personally authenticate them, they would be considered too far-fetched to believe.

One morning in June, 1933, Branham was preparing to teach a Sunday school lesson in Jeffersonville, Indiana. Just before he got up, the Lord had revealed to him seven consecutive visions that would come to pass before the return of Christ. Most have been fulfilled and some are yet to come to pass.

First, Branham saw, and publicly predicted, that Benito Mussolini, the Italian dictator, would establish a fascist state in Italy and invade Ethiopia. Thirty months later the vision came to pass. Branham said the dictator would die a horrible death and his people would spit upon his corpse. This was fulfilled on April 28, 1945 when the people seized the dictator at an airport while he was attempting to escape to Switzerland. He was hung upside down and spit upon by his own people!

In the **second vision** he saw the Siegfried Line two years before it was built. He saw an Austrian named Hitler rising in

Germany, and saw numerous American lives lost in a war with Germany. He predicted Roosevelt would declare war on Germany and would be elected for a fourth term. All of this happened.

The **third vision** revealed three major isms: Fascism, Nazism and Communism. The first two would come to naught but the third, Communism, would flourish. A voice told him to keep his eyes on Russia, because Fascism and Nazism would end up in Communism.

The fourth vision predicted advancement in technology right after the war. He saw automobiles shaped like eggs, and a car with a plastic-looking bubble on top being run by remote control. The driver turned and began playing games with the folks in the back seat.

The **fifth vision** he saw involved women. He witnessed the moral decay of women in America entering into "worldly affairs, bobbing (cutting) their hair and adopting the clothing of men." He then saw women who were stripped nearly naked, covering themselves only with tiny aprons about the size of a fig leaf.

This was 1933, before bikinis, and he saw that they would wear clothes that were far too revealing.

Branham's **sixth vision** involved a woman rising to power in the United States. Branham was quoted as saying:

> *Remember, in that day before the end time comes, a woman—now you all keep this written down. There will be a powerful woman raised up, either to be president or dictator or some great powerful woman in the United States; and (America) will sink under the influence of women.*

On July, 26, 1964, many years later, Branham preached a sermon in which he remarked:

> The morals of our women are going to fall in such degraded things till they're going to be a disgrace to all nations. . . . I saw a woman stand in the United States like a great queen or something. And she was beautiful to look at, but wicked in her heart. She made America's step go with her step.

Because of the accuracy of the prophecies and words of knowledge given to Branham, those who recall these visions are inclined to pay careful attention to them and interpret them in literal terms, not in an allegorical sense. I discussed this sixth vision with a minister who knew Branham personally and traveled with him. He believed the vision could allude to a "Jezebel Spirit" that seizes the church and nation in the future.

After writing down this vision, Branham himself made a note in parenthesis that this woman could be the rise of the Catholic church. Others point out that the wording of the vision mentions a "dictator or a president, or some powerful woman." These words imply more than just a "spirit" or a religious denomination, but an actual female who will sit in great authority in America prior to the return of Christ.

According to the vision, America will morally and spiritually sink during the time of this woman's season of authority.

Note that these events are to unfold prior to the return of Christ. The vision does not indicate whether this woman will rise up before the rapture or before the Second Advent—simply "before the Lord returns."

Even if a woman were elected president, she may not be the woman in this vision, since there will be other elections and opportunities for females to gain the highest position in the land. Since other visions were so accurately fulfilled, it appears this one will also see its completion in the future.

A Biblical correlation may be linked to Jezebel, the first major woman to influence Israel politically in the Bible. Although her husband was king in Samaria, Jezebel controlled all the major decisions. She targeted her hatred toward the ultraconservative prophet, Elijah, who challenged 450 self-appointed prophets of Baal on Mount Carmel.

In this pattern, Ahab was no longer in office and Jezebel remained in the ivory house. In the midst of enjoying security in the ivory palace, judgment came to her, and another took her place (1 Kings 22:39; 2 Kings 9:30-37).

During the reign of Ahab and Jezebel, Elijah the prophet was their thorn in the flesh. After Elijah's departure, Ahab was also gone but Jezebel was still living. She had to deal with Elisha, who had received a double portion of Elijah's anointing (2 Kings 2).

God will always have a voice, a people and a remnant in these final days—especially in America. Only time will tell how and when this sixth vision will play out. When the sixth vision begins to occur, then the seventh and final vision will be on the horizon.

In the **final and seventh vision**, Branham saw a great explosion rend the entire land. It left the United States smoldering and in ruins. He commented that as far as his eyes could see, he saw craters and smoking piles of debris. He said he saw no people in the area of the destruction. Then the vision faded away. This could allude to a final, all-out terror attack on American soil.

Remember, one of the signs of the last days recorded in Scripture is that God will reveal knowledge through dreams and visions (Acts 2:16, 17). Because the other visions came to pass, I believe the final two will be fulfilled in time.

NOTE: Full gospel scholars note that in Branham's later ministry he fell into certain doctrinal error. This sad fact, however, does not take away from his earlier anointing, ministry, and the visions of 1933. Branham was very humble and uneducated, and perhaps was too easily swayed by some who were close to him.

A person's heart can be right with God but their thinking can be wrong doctrinally.

4

America, the New Roman Empire

Doth the eagle mount up at thy command, and make her nest on high (Job 39:27)?

The remarkable link between ancient Israel and America cannot be denied. This spiritual vine is interwoven by God's providence. The olive tree of Israel has the wild branches of the Gentiles grafted in it (Romans 11). But America is more than a spiritual nation. It is a Federal form of government that has its branches linked to another empire, namely the ancient Roman Empire.

The Republic of Rome . . . and America

The prophet Daniel predicted four major world empires from his time until the coming of the Messiah. In retrospect, these empires were Babylon, Media – Persia, Greece and Rome. During Christ's time, the Roman 10th Legion, under the leadership of Titus, destroyed Jerusalem and the Holy Temple in 70 A.D. The Roman Empire is identified in King Nebuchadnezzar's dream in Daniel 2, as two iron legs on a metallic image.

The iron legs represent the division of the Roman Empire between the East and the West. The Eastern headquarters was Constantinople (Istanbul, Turkey); and the Western headquarters was Rome, Italy. This division occurred in the reign of Emperor Constantine. In 1045, another division occurred as the Roman Catholic Church split with the Roman bishops and took control of the western branch and the Eastern branch with its center in Constantinople, Turkey, controlled by the Greek Orthodox.

At the end of days, prior to the return of Christ, 10 kings or rulers will form a united coalition. These are the same 10 kings identified as the ten toes on the image in Daniel 2:42-45. They are also the 10 horns on a beast and the 10 horns on a dragon in Revelation 12 and 13:1-3.

The Roman Empire declined and ceased to exist by the fifth century A.D., and the Holy Roman Empire filled in the gap, as religion and politics mixed to form a system that gave the Roman Church political authority in matters of government. In the late 1800s, there was a decline of the Roman church's control in Europe and a rise of the political authority of the United States and Great Britain. It appears that the United States has filled in the gap and taken on the same patterns of the ancient Roman Empire.

Rome was founded around April 21, 753 B.C. Originally Rome was ruled by seven kings, but eventually they gained independence from the Etruscan kings through a revolt and moved in the direction of a democracy. They established a constitution and became known as a republic (from the Latin word *republica*, meaning "public affairs").

Two traditional political parties formed, one called the *populares*, meaning "people's party," and the other *optimates*, meaning "senatorial party." One claimed to represent the poor people while the other was accused of supporting the rich. The *populares* were considered liberal and the *optimates* were classified as more conservative. Clashes about ideology surfaced between these two parties. In reality, neither party acted on behalf of the poor but only sought the votes of the poor during elections.

Consider the parallels with the formation of America. In the beginning we were ruled and controlled by the kings of England, but broke with them through a revolt called the Revolutionary War. Our independence was sealed with the U.S. Constitution and our nation was called a republic by the founding fathers. A two party system eventually emerged, the Democrats and the Republicans.

During the 20th century, the Democrats claimed to speak for the poorer class and accused the Republicans of being controlled and favored by the rich. The Democrats have become morally more liberal and the Republicans are considered more morally conservative. Some politicians claim to speak for the poorer class, but the sad fact is that they do it for the purpose of gaining a voting bloc among the poor during an election year.

The amazing Roman-American link can be seen in the following correlations:

Both Rome and America were considered superpowers. Rome was the sole superpower during the peak of its empire. In the past Russia and America were considered dueling superpowers. But with the collapse of Communism, America has emerged as the single world power, especially in the realm of economics.

Both Rome and America were considered military powers. Rome was recognized as the mightiest military force in the world. Their soldiers were well-trained with the best equipment in that day. Nations feared the Roman legions, and no country could stand against the Roman soldiers when they gathered en masse against their enemies. America is today recognized globally as the strongest and best military power in the world. America's technology is unsurpassed and our military is the best trained, organized and equipped in the world.

Both occupied the Middle East. The Roman military occupied many nations in the Middle East. America is presently occupying the nations of Afghanistan and Iraq, and has built military bases in Israel. In Roman times, the Romans called Israel Palestine and were in control of the land in the time of Christ.

Both dealt directly with Israel and the Jewish people. The Roman Empire had direct dealings with Israel, just as the American administrations have direct contact and dealings with Israel.

Both had a site called Capitol Hill. The city of Rome had a large hill called in Latin *Capitolina*. From this hill the Roman Senate met to forge laws and pass legislation impacting Roman citizens. In Washington D.C., the Congress and Senate initiate legislation which impacts the lives of American citizens from the U.S. Capitol. The nation's capital is known as "Capitol Hill!"

Both had a Senate. The Roman Empire had a Senate. The United States has a Senate

Both had a main leader. The Romans called the highest official ruling the empire from Rome, *Caesar*. During Paul's ministry, the Caesar was named Nero. He was one of the great persecutors of Christians. Every leader appointed over Rome was called a Caesar. America elects one main leader called a President. Every leader elected to this office received the title, *President of the United States*.

Both had the Eagle as their national emblem. One amazing link is the national emblem. The Roman Empire selected the eagle as their national emblem. The eagle sat atop the military standards of the Roman solders. The United States also selected the eagle as our nation's emblem. The eagle appears on the presidential seal and on all U.S. military seals.

Both experienced slave wars. Slavery was common throughout the world in the time of the Roman Empire. Several revolts among slaves led to several slave wars. America once allowed the purchasing and owning of slaves—until the time of a "revolt" called the Civil War.

Both allowed the killing of infants. At the time of Christ's birth, King Herod instructed the Roman soldiers to enter an area called *Rama* and Bethlehem. They were to slay all of the male children under two years of age because the heathen king heard that a king of the Jews had been born. America has adopted the same spirit of Rome by allowing infants in the wombs of their mothers to be aborted. Both Rome and America show(ed) no respect for the lives of unborn infants.

Both gave freedom to homosexuals. During the time of the apostle Paul, the sin of homosexuality was very strong in the Roman Empire. History reveals that Nero was a homosexual, and that homosexuality was accepted as a normal lifestyle among many of the Roman citizens. In America, the gay lifestyle is called an "alternative lifestyle." This lifestyle is not only acceptable by most Western standards, but is also growing at a rapid rate.

Both had stadiums for sports events. Both Greek and Roman citizens were captivated by sports events, including running, wrestling and chariot racing. These events were often conducted in large stadiums built to accommodate thousands of spectators. America is also a nation filled with stadiums where thousands gather to watch their favorite teams compete. The wrestling industry has become a popular form of violent entertainment in America and the car races have replaced the once popular chariot races of the parallel empire of Rome.

Both people stood when their national anthems were sung in the stadiums. Rome had a national anthem and America has a national anthem. In Rome the anthem was sung in the stadiums and coliseums. Today it is common for the national anthem to be sung in major sporting events prior to the opening of the games.

Both had flags, and pledged their allegiance to their respective flags. In another strange twist, Rome had a special flag that represented the nation. Those faithful to the empire would stand and pledge their allegiance to the national flag. During certain national events, including special military events, it is a tradition for Americans to pledge allegiance to the flag.

Rome eventually turned to eastern cults and religions. Foreign religions found it easy to establish themselves in the empire. Because Rome had no chief religion but welcomed all religions (except Christianity), the people of Rome filled in their spiritual vacuum by turning to eastern cults. Rome had a mixture of spiritual ideas, but did not consider religion as a spiritual experience. Today, Americans are filling their spiritual voids by turning to eastern mysticism, Kabbalah, Hinduism and Buddhism—all eastern religions.

Rome became obsessed with luxuries. Citizens living in Rome became obsessed with finely crafted glass, jewelry and expensive luxuries. It was fashionable to attempt to outdo your neighbor with fancy clothes and "stuff." The same is true with Americans. Parents will pay twice as much just for their children to be seen in "name brand" shoes, clothes and other paraphernalia.

Rome conducted a regular census. Rome conducted a census every five years, and every man had to report the number and names of his family and his slaves. The United States also conducts a national census in which information is recorded concerning family members.

Both Rome and America had a place known as the suburbs. Families usually lived on the outskirts of the city, and both called them suburbs.

As pointed out earlier, the national emblem of the Roman Empire was the Eagle. Cast iron eagles were placed on the military standards of the Roman soldiers, and carved on certain buildings. The correlations continue when comparing certain monuments and goddesses once prominent in the Roman Empire with those sculpted in the United States.

The Statue of Liberty

A large, light-green, metal monument named the Statue of Liberty stands in New York Harbor. Most Americans believe it is simply the statue of a woman holding a torch, welcoming strangers and visitors to America. But in actuality, Lady Liberty herself has existed in tradition for centuries. She is actually the "goddess of liberty," which was worshiped in Rome around 3 B.C. Borrowing her from the Greeks, the ancient Romans placed her likeness on Aventine Hill in the city of Rome.

The statue of Liberty was designed by two Frenchmen who were Free Masons. The Romans borrowed the woman from the Greeks, and several Roman coins were minted with Liberty on their coins. This same woman has been depicted on numerous U.S. postage stamps, and many denominations of our coins have shown her in both side-view and full-figure designs. Statues of Lady Liberty stand atop the domes of the Texas State Capitol in Austin and the Allen County Courthouse in Fort Wayne, Indiana. Lady Liberty is a monument linking Rome with America.

The linkage between Rome and America continues with the design of the U.S. Capitol in Washington, D.C. When the designs were being drawn for the nation's Capitol building, Thomas Jefferson suggested that the building be built in the form of the Roman Pantheon, a building dedicated to all of the ancient gods of Rome.

Eventually the builders settled for a large dome to be mounted in top of the center of the building. In Rome, domes were used to symbolize the unity of the Empire. The name of our Federal building is the Capitol, taken from the Roman name *Capitolinum*. The Roman name for a domed structure is *Capitolinum*. One early document even calls our capitol building the Temple of Liberty.

Many of the major federal government buildings constructed in Washington, D.C., are made from marble and stone, using the same architecture from the Roman and Greek periods. Huge columns of Roman design tower above the porches in the same manner as the buildings constructed in both Rome and Greece.

Rome's Decline and the Decline of America

Centuries ago, the mighty Roman Empire controlled the military power, economic authority and trade routes among the nations in and around the Mediterranean Sea. For several hundred years, it seemed Rome would dominate forever. This, however, did not happen. The Empire fell into a moral abyss which led to its eventual disappearance from history and replacement by other empires and nations.

It is important to note that the moral and spiritual decline now occurring in the United States has many parallels with the decline of the Roman Empire.

The Roman Military and Pax Romana

The Roman Empire was noted for its strong, dominating military. The Empire had established *Pax Romana*, or Roman peace. The purpose of *Pax Romana* was to keep the citizens tranquil throughout the Empire. Roman soldiers were stationed to protect the borders of nations, squelch civil uprisings and defeat rebellions that arose in the form of revolts against Roman troops. The troops were considered by some, including many Jews in Israel, as occupiers.

Roman soldiers spent countless weeks in physical and mental training to ensure they were a well-oiled fighting machine. The army gave a number and rank to each of their legions. The men were paid for their training and rewarded for their victories. Special necklaces and armbands were given to the soldiers, and embossed disks were worn on their uniforms. There was even an army of engineers to service roads and bridges! Needless to say, the occupation of lands, putting down uprisings among rebels and guarding the borders cost huge amounts of money. As a result, the government incurred mounting debt.

To increase the revenue for the government, the taxes kept increasing for the general public. The higher the debt, the more taxes were raised. Evidence of global taxation is recorded in the Bible at the time of Christ's birth. Luke says, "There went out a decree from Caesar Augustus that all the world should be taxed" (Luke 2:1). This taxation began to affect the personal salaries of the common workers. The government was taxing income more frequently and workers "take-home pay" was becoming less.

Eventually, once-prosperous farmers could not repay their bills and loans, so they threw up their hands and quit. So many Roman farmers were unwilling or unable to work that the government developed a welfare system that distributed doles. A bankrupt farmer had one of three choices:

1. Join the Roman army. In this manner a man would receive a steady salary and food.

2. Go to a new land where the population was low, colonize it and build his fortunes from the start.

3. Go on the welfare rolls and depend on government doles (subsidies).

As taxes went up, more Romans left their jobs, being unable to survive. The welfare system began as a good initiative, but eventually became a burden and a heavy load on the government, as the masses became dependent on government assistance. The burden to provide taxes fell on the well-to-do as the government demanded they bear the brunt of the taxes.

Eventually the middle class of Roman society was squeezed out of existence; the burden fell on the government. Today in America we hear the cry from Washington that the government needs more tax revenues, and the well-to-do need to pay more taxes!

The Declining Birth Rate of the Empire

As taxes rose, births declined. Couples could no longer afford to have children. This impacted the leaders of the Senate. Under Nero, 400 senators lost their family lineage and heritage because they had no children to carry on their names. As the estates and farms were placed on the public market, the rich began to purchase them for their estates. By the year A.D. 100, there were 2,000 land owners in all of Italy. It may be that the reason the Romans invaded Jerusalem, destroying the Temple, was to seize the gold and silver vessels and take them to Rome, thus increasing their wealth.

The Temple in Jerusalem was the one place where the treasuries were filled with gold, silver and precious things. In the year A.D. 70, General Titus broke through the strong walls of Jerusalem but gave instructions to his soldiers to not destroy the sacred Temple. A soldier, however, threw a torch into a window, and eventually the inner sanctuary was on fire. The fire was so great that the gold within the Holy Temple melted and ran down the stone walls.

When the dust settled and the fires ceased, the soldiers toppled the stones in order to peel off the gold that had dripped down the stones. The holy and sacred treasures, such as the silver trumpets, the golden Menorah and precious things, were brought, in a triumphant procession, into the city of Rome to the cheering crowds.

The invasion however was not enough to undergird the economic crisis that had enveloped the government. As time passed, the military began to decline, as soldiers became slothful and unconcerned with their assignments. Careless living, a love for luxuries, and complacency eventually cost the empire its global control.

Six More Rome-America Parallels

As we continue to connect the dots between the early Roman dominion and America, the almost unbelievable parallels continue:

1. The Romans filled stadiums for their sports events.

During the Roman Empire, Sunday became just another day to work and to fill the stadiums for the many sporting events. Years ago in America, most stores were closed on Sunday to give employees opportunity to attend worship services and proved a much needed day of rest. Today, Sunday is no longer the Lord's day but is another day in which Americans golf, go to the malls and fill stadiums for games.

2. The Roman athletes were highly paid and exalted in the public arena.

Roman athletes were paid more than almost any other group in the empire. A successful athlete was granted special privileges. In America, professional athletes are often paid huge amounts of money for their performance. Often, if a noted athlete is arrested for alcohol, drug use or some criminal act, some are often pressured to exonerate them, perhaps to avoid a negative impact on the particular sport.

3. The Romans were tolerant of every god from every nation except the God of Christianity.

The Romans allowed various gods to be worshiped within the Empire. They were tolerant of all religions except Christianity. Roman leaders clashed with Christians because Christians refused to call the Roman Emperor, *God*. Christians would not participate in Rome's pagan holidays. Christians had also set aside a day to worship Jesus, and this required allowing them off of work, thus causing an ongoing conflict. As a result, the Christians were targeted for persecution and were hated among many in the Roman political system.

Although America was founded as a Christian nation tolerant of every other religion, the Christian population is beginning to experience increasing opposition from organizations such as the ACLU, who are attempting to remove the freedom to practice the Christian faith from all public places. As long as a so-called minister sugarcoats the gospel, hides the Cross, never tells a lost person he is a sinner and ignores the fact that Christ is the only way to heaven, he is considered tolerant and his church will grow.

Christians who are firm in their beliefs and who will not deny the faith and the Cross are ridiculed as right-wing religious fanatics, and are accused of being intolerant of others. This scenario is a repeat of the Roman Empire.

4. Roman tax money supported infant murder.

Most Americans cannot comprehend the idea a government could permit children from two years of age and under to be slaughtered alive by the swords of Roman soldiers. Yet, Herod the Great initiated a door-to-door holocaust where all male children under age two were killed. All Americans would be stunned and appalled if the federal government initiated genocide of children under two years of age.

Yet, a large percentage of the population permits, and supports, abortion on demand. Roman tax money paid the soldiers who slew the children in and around Bethlehem, just as our tax dollars pay for the abortion of infants in America.

5. Rome allowed same-sex relations in its empire.

Rome was considered tolerant toward all forms of sexual activities, including same-sex relationships. One of the most wicked emperors of all time was Nero, who ruled at the time of the apostle Paul. Nero was a schizophrenic and participated in drunken orgies at his palace in Rome, including engaging in homosexual activity. Hot baths were a part of Roman culture, which were, in reality, hotbeds for male and female prostitution.

In the name of tolerance, Americans have permitted, allowed and accepted the gay lifestyle among both men and women. Major cities host parties and parades where men flaunt their "sexual preferences" publicly, while "straight" Americans turn their heads and go on with life.

6. Roman sports became more violent and bloody.

Roman athletics moved from the Greek form of the games to the more violent and bloody sports, including gladiator fighting at the arena. The fights were not staged, but were well organized and very deadly. Eventually, the hatred for Christians led to the blood sport of feeding the Christians to the wild animals in the Roman coliseum. Crowds were worked into a frenzy, as the arena was rocked by the jeering and shouting multitudes.

America was once content with three basic sports: baseball, football and basketball. Today, however, many in America are turning to more violent and bloody sports, some of which are classified as "entertainment."

Will America face the same internal moral and spiritual deterioration that came to Rome? If we follow the same course, we will arrive at the same destination. Biblical prophecy indicates the final empire will rise in the region around the Mediterranean Sea. For this to come to pass, America may not be in the picture. The return of the Lord for the church may initiate the decline of America and a major re-alignment of the nations of the world.

Some voices contend that "the jig is up" for America. They say that we as a nation had might as well throw in the towel. Quit! Give it up! Forget about everything! America is fast "going to hell in a hand basket," they assert, and there's nothing we can do about it. So we'd might as well draw up in a little cocoon and do nothing.

Others allege that we are approaching a New World Order (NWO) in which nations will coexist with each other in peace. There will be global turmoil until the NWO is in place; then, presto, everything will be fine. Unprecedented prosperity is just ahead, they contend, if we will only submit meekly to their agendas and their leaders.

God's people see the world from a different perspective, however. You and I listen to the many newscasts and read the regular news reports. We are appalled to see the reports of America's declining influence in the world theater. We see the "photo-op" scenes of disrespect to our flag and our citizens. Although we know that some of these displays are staged, the sad truth remains that America's role in world events is not as all-pervasive as it once was. What is happening? We read the Bible along with the daily newspapers. We see prophecy being fulfilled as we observe the kaleidoscope of news events playing out on the television screen. We see the stage being set for the playing out of the great drama of the Revelation. But we see these things with hope and with growing excitement:

> *For the grace of God that brings salvation has appeared . . . teaching us that, denying ungodliness and worldly lusts, we should live soberly, righteously, and godly in the present age, looking for the blessed hope and glorious appearing of our great God and Savior Jesus Christ* (Titus 2:11-13).

The moral decline of the Roman Empire teaches us that we must undergird and protect the family unit. The strength and security of the home are determined by the relationships built by a caring mother and father. Presently, the sons and daughters of the family unit are under severe assault. Understanding the Ishmael spirit may open our eyes to the enemy's plan of attack against the home.

5

The Ishmael Spirit in the American Home

He shall be a wild man; his hand shall be against every man, and every man's hand against him. And he shall dwell in the presence of all his brethren (Genesis 16:12).

A portrait of the American family could be the central feature in a history museum a hundred years from now—if the present deterioration of the family continues. The God-ordained family unit was the Almighty's method of passing blessings from one generation to the next. The breakup of the home creates stress, financial burdens, anger and a generation of youth who often turn against the faith of their parents and grandparents.

A major shortage in America is a daddy shortage. Too many men have gone AWOL from their own children who were born in their image and likeness. The tragedy is that it is the children who suffer.

~ Half of all marriages in America end in divorce.

~ Half of the children in America live with a single parent.

~ Single girls become pregnant and raise the child without the father.

~ Fathers are leaving their families to live a lifestyle of fornication and promiscuity.

When children have no father figure, they will seek something or someone to fill the void. During World War I, millions of young men lost their lives in battle. Children throughout Europe were fatherless and without brothers and cousins. Communism sought to fill the gap as Stalin became the father figure for the masses.

World War II followed as millions fought again throughout Europe. The loss of men created another void in the homes of mothers and wives. Suddenly, Germany became the mother and Hitler the father of a new German race the dictator dreamed of forming. The youth of Germany pledged their souls, bodies and hearts to their new father.

In Islam, a Muslim man can have up to five wives at a time, and as many children as he desires. While the children may call him father, the religion of Islam becomes the actual father of the family. In nations such as Sudan, millions of men have been murdered, leaving behind wives, daughters and children.

Ishmael—the Wounded Teenager

Ishmael is an example of the type of person a child becomes when he is separated from his father. Ishmael was the son of

Abraham (Genesis 16:15). His mother was an Egyptian handmaiden who served Abraham's wife, Sarah. For 13 years Ishmael was Abraham's only son. He had the full attention and affection of Abraham.

After Sarah became pregnant, she demanded that Hagar and Ishmael be expelled from the house (Genesis 21:14). I can only imagine the grief and pain the mother and son experienced. The separation from his biological father birthed a bitter feeling in the young lad. That bitterness is evident today between the sons of Isaac (Israel) and the sons of Ishmael (the Arabs).

Armed with the clothes on their backs and a bottle of water, they both became stranded in a desert, suffering from heat exhaustion.

> *The water in the skin was used up, and she placed the boy under one of the shrubs. Then she went and sat down across from him at a distance of about a bowshot; for she said to herself, "Let me not see the death of the boy." So she sat opposite him, and lifted her voice and wept* (Genesis 21:15, 16).

As Hagar cried out, God provided a well of water to sustain the single mom and her son. Ishmael survived, living in the desert as an archer. God spoke these words over the young man:

> *He shall be a wild man; his hand shall be against every man, and every man's hand against him. And he shall dwell in the presence of all his brethren* (Genesis 16:12).

The word *wild* in Hebrew means to "run wild." It is used to describe a wild donkey. God was saying that Ishmael would have no stability. He would be like a wild donkey that no one can control. He would be a man of contention and conflict with others, because his "hand shall be against every man."

Without fatherly instruction in his teen years, Ishmael became uncontrollable and had no respect for others.

The same wild spirit can be detected in many of our major cities. Gangs of youths roam the alleys and streets, robbing, fighting, maiming and killing. Their hands are against every person who is not in their group. No one can control them. Fear rules. So many young men in this Ishmael generation end up getting hooked on drugs and eventually spend time in prison.

Dad and God

Most Christian psychologists believe a child compares the nature and love of God with that of his or her father. If dad is always angry, then God is mad all the time. If dad is continually punishing the child, God is always seeking revenge. If dad is never home, then God is never there when you need him. Should dad be lazy, the reflection is that God doesn't really care.

If dad, however, is a caring, affectionate and loving father, then his nature becomes a reflection of the nature of God in the mind of the child. Without a male in the life of the child, something or someone else will fill in the gap. Too often, the lack of male attention causes young girls to seek attention from young men who are all too often immature and self-serving. She enters a serious relationship, becomes physically involved and is dumped in a few weeks, only to suffer pain again.

I believe one reason there is much homosexuality in the nation is the fathers are AWOL from the family. Why has homosexuality and lesbianism become so widespread in our time? I believe something is seriously lacking in the church, society and home that has caused this increase. Often a young woman who has been wounded by men (dad, husband or relative), connects with other women and soon an unhealthy emotional bond is forged. Many young men who tend toward the gay lifestyle have effeminate actions and are mocked as weak and "sissy." At times they are seeking strong male affirmation because they are not receiving it through normal family channels.

The Curse of Benjamin

In Israel's early history, there was a tribe that almost lost its entire heritage. At a certain point in Benjamin's history, the men of that tribe became almost completely engrossed in same-sex relationships. Disgusted with their behavior, the other 11 tribes decreed that no one could allow his daughter to marry a man from Benjamin. The behavior of some of these homosexual men, who were also guilty of rape, so incensed the rest of Israel that it provoked a civil war. Thousands were slain, but the Tribe of Benjamin was defeated.

After the war, cooler heads prevailed. Judges 21 records how the word came forth from the other tribes that permitted the men of Benjamin to marry women, so that their seed would be carried on and their tribe would not be destroyed. I'm sure that later on, King Saul in the Old Testament and the apostle Paul in the New Testament (both of whom were from this tribe), were grateful that the tribe had not been completely destroyed years before.

In a television debate between a "gay" man and a "straight" Christian, the gay man said there was no place in the Bible where the word *homosexual* was used, and no direct reference which forbade a same-sex relationship. While it is true the word homosexual is not in the English translation of the Bible, the sexual activity between the same sexes is forbidden:

> *You shall not lie with a man as with a woman. This is an abomination* (Leviticus 18:22).

Sexual immorality is strongly forbidden in both the Old and New Testaments. This includes adultery, fornication, incest, rape, beastiality and homosexuality. Many nations participated in terrible idolatry and sexual sins in Bible times, and were judged by God (Leviticus 18:24, 25). God warned the Hebrews that they too would encounter His wrath if they followed the same path of the ungodly (Leviticus 18:26-30). Under the Old Covenant certain types of sexual sins were punishable by death.

> *If a man lies with a male as he lies with a woman, both of them have committed an abomination. They shall surely be put to death. Their blood shall be upon them* (Leviticus 20:13).

Some may say these warnings were in the Old Testament, and we are under the New Testament guidelines. Let's view the warnings given in the New Testament. Paul wrote:

> *Do you not know that the unrighteous will not inherit the kingdom of God? Do not be deceived. Neither fornicators, nor idolaters, nor effeminate, nor abusers of themselves with mankind, nor thieves, nor covetous, nor drunkards, nor revilers, nor extortioners will inherit the kingdom of God* (1 Corinthians 6:9, 10).

The word *effeminate* in Greek is *malakok*, which means "a male who submits his body for unnatural lewdness" (Thayer's). The term "abusers of themselves with mankind" in Greek is *arenokoitai*, which means "one who lies with a male as a female" (Thayer's). This clearly speaks of sexual immorality in the form of homosexuality. "Not inheriting the kingdom" alludes to not spending eternity with God in His eternal kingdom.

Paul also wrote these words:

Such were some of you. But now you are washed, but now you are sanctified, now you are justified in the name of the Lord Jesus and by the Spirit of God (1 Corinthians 6:11).

Paul was writing to the Christians in Rome, a city controlled by Nero, a persecutor of the Christian faith. His words promise hope and deliverance, through Jesus Christ, for someone bound in a sinful lifestyle! However, he firmly warned the disobedient in Romans 1:18, 21-28:

For the wrath of God is revealed from heaven against all ungodliness and unrighteousness of men, who suppress the truth in unrighteousness.

Because, although they knew God, they did not glorify Him as God, nor were thankful, but became futile in their thoughts, and their foolish hearts were darkened. Professing to be wise, they became fools, and changed the glory of the incorruptible God into an image made like corruptible man—and birds and four-footed animals and creeping things.

Therefore God also gave them up to uncleanness, in the lusts of their hearts, to dishonor their bodies among themselves, who exchanged the truth of God for the lie, and worshiped and served the creature rather than the Creator, who is blessed forever. Amen.

For this reason God gave them up to vile passions. For even their women exchanged the natural use for what is against nature. Likewise also the men, leaving the natural use of the woman, burned in

*their lust for one another, men with men committing
what is shameful, and receiving in themselves the
penalty of their error which was due.*

*And even as they did not like to retain God in their
knowledge, God gave them over to a debased mind,
to do those things which are not fitting.*

Three times Paul said, "God gave them over," because they
became vain in their imaginations.

The Early Fathers

Were same-sex relationships permitted in the early church?
How did the early fathers of Christianity view men with men
and women with women? According to their statements, this
sexual problem was also prevailing in their time, even among
some in the church. The fathers wrote these views:

THEOPHILUS OF ANTIOCH, A.D. 180

*For the unbelieving and the contemptuous, and for
those who do not submit to the truth but assent to
iniquity, when they have been involved in adulteries,
and fornications, and homosexualities, and avarice,
and in lawless idolatries, there will be wrath and
indignation, tribulation and anguish; and in the end,
such men as these will be detained in everlasting
fire* (To Autolycus 1:14).

TERTULLIAN, A.D. 220

*All frenzies of the lust which exceed the laws of
nature, and are impious toward both (human) bodies*

and the sexes, we banish, not only from the threshold but also all shelter of the church, for they are not sins so much as monstrosities (Modesty 4).

BASIL THE GREAT, A.D. 367

He who is guilty of unseemliness with males will be under the same discipline for the same time as adulterers (Letters 217:62).

If you (O, monk) are young in either body or mind, shun the companionship of other young men and avoid them as you would a flame. For through them the enemy has kindled desires of many then handed them over to eternal fire, hurling them into the vile pit of the five cities under the pretense of spiritual love (The Renunciation of the World).

JOHN CHRYSOSTOM, A.D. 391

(Certain men in the church) come in gazing at the beauty of women; others curious about the blooming youth of boys. After this, do you not marvel that lightning bolts are not launched (from heaven), and all these things are not plucked up from their foundation? For worthy both of thunderbolts and hell are the things that are done; but God, who is longsuffering, and of great mercy, forbears awhile his wrath, calling you to repentance and amendment (Homily on Matthew 3:3).

All of these affections ...were vile, but chiefly the mad lust after males: for the soul is more the sufferer in sins and more dishonored than the body in diseases. The men have done an insult to nature itself (Romans 1:26, 27) (Homily on Romans 4).

Augustine, A.D 400.

Those shameful acts against nature, such as were committed in Sodom, ought everywhere and always to be detested and punished. If all nations were to do such things, they would be held guilty of the same crime by the law of God which has not made men so that they should use one another in this way (Apostolic Constitutions 6:11).

It is clear from the Scripture and from the early fathers that same-sex relations were both wrong and eventually led to eternal punishment. While this is strong teaching and is rejected by today's society, the destruction of Sodom and Gomorrah, as you will learn, is an example and a warning.

The story of Ishmael correlates with the lives of countless youths in America. This fatherless generation creates sad consequences and broken hearts for sons and daughters. The church must arise and fill in the gap by loving, respecting and teaching this generation to avoid the misplaced affection that leads to same-sex relationships. We must preach that God loves the sinner, but not the sin; and must continue to warn the Ishmael generation of the consequences of wrong choices. Otherwise, our nation will find itself in the same line of fire as the cities of Sodom and Gomorrah (Genesis 19:1-28).

6

The Ghost of Sodom
Is Rising Again

If history repeats itself, then history will repeat both the good and the bad. The people of the ancient cities of the Middle East became filled with idolatry, fornication, beastiality and homosexuality. Although these Biblical cities are buried underneath tons of dirt and debris, the spirit of those tragic cities is reviving in our nation. The ancient ghost of Sodom is rising again.

Liberal theology and secular "Christians" are offended when a minister preaches the danger of following the sins of ancient empires. Often they say, "That's just some story from the Old Testament and we live in a different time." Perhaps the warnings penned by Peter and Jude make the case for continually reminding the super-seeker-sensitive believers in North America.

As Sodom and Gomorrah, and the cities around them in a similar manner to these, having given themselves over to sexual immorality and gone after strange flesh, are set forth as an example, suffering the vengeance of eternal fire (Jude 7).

And turning the cities of Sodom and Gomorrah into ashes, condemned them to destruction, making them an example to those who afterward would live ungodly (2 Peter 2:6).

The destruction of the city of Sodom was an example to future generations. If any nation follows the example of the men of Sodom, God makes it clear that the nation can, and eventually will, receive the same punishment for their sins. The 21st century has witnessed a revival of immorality and an emphasis on special rights, including the right for gay men and women to marry someone of their same sex and adopt children. The question is often asked, "Where did this type of sin originate?" The answer appears to be, "After the flood of Noah."

The Curse of Canaan

Years following the universal flood, Noah planted a vineyard and became drunk with the wine from it. The Bible tells us that in this drunken condition, he was uncovered (naked), lying in his tent (Genesis 9:21). Noah's son, Ham, entered the tent and saw his father's nude body. He immediately told his two brothers, who had entered the tent backwards, to cover their father (Genesis 9:23).

When Noah awoke, the Scripture says, he "knew what his younger son had done." He then said, "Cursed be Canaan; a servant of servants shall he be" (Genesis 9:25). For years Christians taught that Ham was cursed, but no place in the

Bible teaches this. Also, Ham was not the younger son of Noah, he was the second son, according to the listing in Genesis 5:32; 7:13 and 10:1. Who was the "younger son?" It was the youngest son of Ham, Canaan. Noah never cursed Ham, but he did curse Canaan, the youngest son of Ham (Genesis 10:6).

Why did Noah curse Canaan? Noah was drunk and naked in his tent. Some Hebrew scholars believe that Canaan went into the tent of his grandfather and performed a homosexual act on him while he was drunk. After waking, Noah realized what had happen and pronounced a curse on Canaan.

According to the Word of God, Canaan and his sons eventually settled in a land known as Canaan land. This region of the country was filled with several descendants of Canaan who had formed large tribes and were identified as the Canaanites. A list in found in Genesis 10:15-19.

~ The Jebusite

~ The Amorite

~ The Hivite

~ The Arkite

~ The Sinite

~ The Arvadite

~ The Zemarite

~ The Hamathite

~ The Girgasite

Further insight from Jewish religious literature, the book of Jasher, reveals more detail about the children of Canaan. Several of his descendants built cities in the land. Several of these cities are mentioned in the Bible:

The children of Canaan also built themselves cities, and they called their cities after their names, eleven

> *cities and others without number. And four men*
> *from the family of Ham went to the land of the*
> *plain; these were the names of the four men,*
> *Sodom, Gomorrah, Admah and Zeboyim. These men*
> *built four cities in the land of the plain, and they*
> *called the names of their cities after their own names*
> (Jasher 10: 24-26).

The four cities, Sodom, Gomorrah, Admah, and Zeboyim, are named in the Bible as cities of the plain. This was an area in ancient Israel located near the southern part of the Dead Sea (Genesis 14:2). Canaan's descendants built these cities, and it appears that many in his family lineage were affected by the same "generational curse" as their ancestor.

Sodom was a city filled with homosexual activity to such an extent that Lot was grieved every day because of the filthiness of the wicked there. What he saw and heard vexed his soul (2 Peter 2:7). The writings in Jasher add more insight into the wickedness of Sodom. The laws passed by the four judges opened the door to all forms of sexual perversion.

> *And the cities of Sodom had four judges to four*
> *cities, and these were their names, Serak in the*
> *city of Sodom, Sharkad in Gomorrah, Zabnac in*
> *Admah, and Menon in Zeboyim* (Jasher 19:1).
>
> *And by the desire of their four judges the people of*
> *Sodom and Gomorrah had beds erected in the*
> *streets of the cities, and if a man came to these*
> *places they laid hold of him and brought him to one*
> *of their beds, and by force made him to lie in them*
> (Jasher 19:3).

Not only was the sin of Canaan transferred through his family seed living in Canaan land, but the judges passed laws where men could lay beds in the streets and have relations with other men. No wonder God said, "The cry of Sodom and Gomorrah is great . . . because their sin is very grave" (Genesis 18:20).

When it came time for Lot to be evacuated from the city of Sodom, he requested to flee up the mountain to a small city called Zoar. Permission was given and when the four vile cities were cremated, Zoar was spared (Genesis 19:19-22). The book of Jasher does not mention Zoar having a judge. The same laws were not passed in the smaller city, but were popular and accepted among the larger, more "liberal-minded and tolerant" citizens of the four larger cities.

Return to Sodom

It appears that the ghost of Sodom is rising again. When the city existed, both young and old men were involved in sexual immorality (Genesis 19:5). These lust-filled individuals would come out at night, searching the streets for male strangers they could molest or rape (Genesis 19:5). Their wickedness and bondage was so intense, that the rioters attempted to tear down the door of Lot's house to gain access to two male strangers who were spending the night there (Genesis 19:6).

In a somewhat shocking offer, Lot told the mob he had two daughters who were virgins, and they could take his daughters and do whatever they wished. He begged them to leave the strangers alone. This passage troubled me for years, until I realized that Lot knew the men were so vile they were not interested in women. Their craving was for men only. Had it not been for the supernatural intervention of two angels, Lot himself would have become a victim of the predators.

> And they said, "Stand back!" Then they said, "This one came in to stay here, and he keeps acting as a

> *judge; now we will deal worse with you than with them." So they pressed hard against the man Lot, and came near to break down the door* (Genesis 19:9).

Certain cities in our nation host large marches and celebrations for those who practice the same sexual lifestyle. One such city is San Francisco, California. Years ago, a minister distributed a video showing a major gay rally. I was grieved to see signs that read, "God is Gay," and, "Jesus says gay is cool." Others were dressed like nuns and Catholic priests, as they performed vulgar acts on the streets in public in broad daylight.

One day before New Orleans would have hosted a homosexual celebration by a group that calls themselves Southern Decadence, Hurricane Katrina hit the gulf coast, devastating the city. For 35 years, this group had met in New Orleans on the Sunday before Labor Day. Tens of thousands of gay men dressed in drag and clogged the city streets. Publicity advertising the event told how the "whole drunken, rowdy group weaves its drunken way down the streets of the [French] Quarter, one year cutting through Saint Louis Basilica during Mass."

In 2005, the group was expecting 125,000 people to attend this gay celebration and bring $100 million dollars with them to the city. On the planned week of the march, however, the city was lying in ruins and under water. Prior to the event they boasted, "Not even the fire from the dragon's breath would keep participants and watchers from assembling in the 1200 block of Royal Street." Not fire from a "dragon," but water from a flood cancelled the event for the first time in 35 years!

The New Testament warned that Sodom was destroyed as an example to those who would follow in the same sins. While Christians love all sinners and those who do not know Christ, we cannot tolerate the promotion and practice of vile iniquity. We know this will bring the disfavor of God to the nation.

The judges of Sodom were responsible for passing laws that led to the spiritual and moral deterioration of the citizens. During recent years, judges in America have tragically legislated from the bench and inserted their personal social opinions into the law, instead of defending the law. From prayer and Bible reading being removed from public places to the approval of same-sex marriage, the judges have failed the righteous people in this nation.

The Balaam Strategy Against America

If righteous people do not wake up, speak up, stand up and pray up, we may find ourselves falling for the Balaam strategy. This is a plan designed to bring the disfavor of God on the nation. The strange story of Balaam's manipulation, found in Numbers 22-24, should serve as a warning to us.

Balaam, an Old Testament prophet and seer, had a unique gift. He could see into the future and speak words that would come to pass. He was hired by Balak, the King of Moab, to place a verbal curse on the Hebrews after they fled Egypt. Balaam stood to curse Israel, but only words of blessing flowed out of his mouth. In frustration, the Moab king sought to know how he could curse the Hebrews. Balaam's compromise led to his demise.

The prophet gave the king a strategy to bring the beautiful women of Moab into the camp of Israel, instructing the women to seduce the men. This action was a sin to the Hebrew God, the prophet said, and would bring a curse against them. The plan was effective. As Jewish men yielded to temptation and practiced fornication with the Moabite beauties, God became angry and sent a terrible plague that spread throughout the camp. Because Balaam "set up" God's elect, his name is always negative throughout the Bible.

> *Behold, these women caused the children of Israel, through the counsel of Balaam, to commit trespass against the Lord . . . and there was a plague among the congregation of the Lord* (Numbers 31:16).

> *But I have a few things against you, because you have . . . those who hold the doctrine of Balaam, who taught Balak to put a stumbling block before the children of Israel . . . to commit sexual immorality* (Revelation 2:14).

Balaam's strategy was a stumbling block. The Greek word is *skandelon*, meaning "a trap, or a snare set for a person." America is a great nation, blessed by the hand of Providence. The Creator planned our beginnings and placed in the hearts of the founders a spiritual desire to make a Christian nation. Millions of true, God-fearing Christians are scattered like lights in the darkness across the nation. Because of the number of the righteous people, Satan is unable to curse this nation.

If God would have spared Sodom for 10 righteous people, America has far more than 10 who are righteous. I believe Satan's plan is to blind the righteous into accepting sin as an option without consequences. This attitude would raise the anger of God against His own people and force God's hand to judge our nation. As Peter said, "And if the righteous scarcely be saved, where shall the ungodly and the sinner appear (1 Peter 4:18)? Recent prophetic signs in America may be an early warning, such as the signs of tsunamis and hurricanes.

7

The Sea Is Roaring and the Cities Are Shaking

The nations will rush like the rushing of many waters; but God will rebuke them and they will flee far away, and be chased like the chaff of the mountains before the wind, like a rolling thing before the whirlwind. Then behold, at eventide, trouble! And before the morning, he is no more. This is the portion of those who plunder us, and the lot of those who rob us (Isaiah 17:13, 14).

The attack of 9/11 was called the worst tragedy on American soil since Pearl Harbor and the worst terrorist attack in America's history. But that was before the killer hurricane that struck the coasts of Louisiana, Alabama and Mississippi. Former President Clinton said the devastation from Hurricane Katrina was worse than the devastation caused by the 9/11 attacks.

Why did God allow this storm? Could He not have stopped it before it struck? Why did God allow so many churches and so many Christians' homes to be destroyed, along with the casinos, strip clubs and voodoo shops? Was this storm just another natural disaster, a storm cycle, or a chastisement from God? These questions cause a rift among ministers and pastors. To balance positive faith with an understanding of God's judgment on sin, ministers often skirt this issue, or stand on opposite sides of the ring and attack those who hold an opposing view as to why God allowed such destruction.

All Men Suffer at Times

It must be clearly understood that suffering is a part of living. Human suffering comes in different forms at different times. It may be in the form of a separation, a death or a divorce. It may be a loss caused by a job layoff, or a violent hurricane. From the cradle to the grave, at some point all humans will feel pain; life will seem unfair. "Man is born to trouble as surely as the sparks fly upward" (Job 5:7).

Living in the End Times

Living in the end times is exciting; however, we must understand that certain prophecies will be fulfilled in our time. Some of these predictions are not always pleasant. We love the precious promises, but want to shun the painful prophecies. We must not ignore the warnings but instead, must discern their meanings. Jesus gave such a prediction in Luke 21:25:

> And there will be signs in the sun, in the moon, and in the stars; and on the earth distress of nations, with perplexity, the sea and the waves roaring.

Notice how four other Bible translations render this passage:

And there will be signs in the sun and moon and stars; and upon the earth [there will be] distress (trouble and anguish) of nations in bewilderment and perplexity [without resources, left wanting, embarrassed, in doubt, not knowing which way to turn] at the roaring (echo) of the tossing of the sea (AMP).

Then there will be signs in the sun, moon, and stars; and there will be anguish on the earth among nations bewildered by the roaring sea and waves (HCSB).

There will be signs in the sun and moon and stars, and on the earth dismay among nations, in perplexity at the roaring of the sea and the waves (NASB).

And there will be strange events in the skies—signs in the sun, moon, and stars. And down here on earth the nations will be in turmoil, perplexed by the roaring seas and strange tides (NLT).

Each translation emphasizes that trouble will arise from the sea in the form of waves and billows. The phrase *sea and the waves roaring* indicates a noise from the water. The word *roaring* in Greek is "echo." During the 2004 tsunami which struck the Pacific Rim, survivors stated they heard a "roaring sound coming from the sea!" A roaring echo can be heard in a major hurricane as the winds claw through the elements. What we have witnessed in the tsunami and the hurricanes fit the imagery given in Christ's warning.

In this same passage, Jesus indicated that nations would be in perplexity, not knowing a way out or not knowing what to do because of the agitation of the sea and the waves. This is certainly true. Americans have now witnessed how a major hurricane in a major city does more than destroy buildings.

The aftermath produces shortages of water, food and fuel; and can birth disease and famine.

In 2004, the State of Florida was hit by four hurricanes, causing stress and great sorrow to many citizens who were stretched almost beyond human limitations. No wonder Christ said men's hearts would fail them because of fear, and looking after what would come to pass on the earth.

A Repeat of Noah's Days

A second observation concerns the correlations with the days of Noah. Christ said that "as the days of Noah *were*, so also will the coming of the Son of Man be" (Matthew 24:37). Noah was 10 generations from Adam. Josephus writes that Adam's son, Seth, and his sons, recorded a warning in brick and stone concerning the destruction of the earth by water and fire:

> *They (Seth's sons) also were the inventors of that peculiar sort of wisdom which is concerned with the heavenly bodies and their order. And that their inventions might not be lost before they were sufficiently known, upon Adam's prediction that the world was to be destroyed at one time by the force of fire and at another time by the violence and quantity of water, they made two pillars; one of brick and the other of stone: they inscribed their discoveries on them both, that in case the brick might be destroyed by the flood, the pillar of stone might remain, and exhibit these discoveries to mankind; and also to inform them that there was another pillar of brick erected by them. Now this remains in the land of Siriad to this day* (Josephus, *Antiquities of the Jews,* II.3).

The prediction of water covering the earth was fulfilled in Noah's time. In the Genesis account, two major things produced the flood waters. The "fountains of the great deep were broken up, and the windows of heaven were opened" (Genesis 7:11). Water was pouring from two different places.

The word "deep" is the Hebrew word *tehom*, which alludes to underground chambers in the earth that hold springs and rivers. At the moment of the flood, the earth began to split and the waters underground began gushing out. The windows of heaven, alludes to the rain coming from the sky.

This is a perfect picture of both the tsunami and the hurricanes. The tsunami was caused by a major earthquake which occurred when the plates under the Pacific Rim shifted and a massive tidal wave was created. This underwater rift was over 780 miles long under the sea. The "fountains of the great deep were broken!"

Hurricanes are a result of the wind and rain coming from heaven. We look at both of these tragedies and say they are signs of the "Days of Noah" being repeated in our day and time.

Heeding the Warnings

Scriptures reveal that God visits in mercy before He visits in judgment. Prior to His judgment, He often warns His people, giving them an opportunity to escape the coming trouble. An example is Matthew 24. The disciples were bragging on the beauty of the Temple in Jerusalem when Jesus warned:

> *And Jesus said to them, "Do you not see all these things? Assuredly, I say to you, not one stone shall be left here upon another, that shall not be thrown down"* (Matthew 24:2).

This was a shocking prediction, since the Temple had previously been destroyed by the Babylonians 600 years prior. Later, Christ revealed a sign they would see, indicating the timing of the disaster. He told His followers what to do when they saw Jerusalem surrounded by armies:

> *Let those who are in Judea flee to the mountains. Let him who is on the housetop not go down to take anything out of his house. And let him who is in the field not go back to get his clothes. But woe to those who are pregnant and to those who are nursing babies in those days* (Matthew 24:16-19).

Four important elements are contained in this prediction.

~ First, He said to get out of the city immediately and head to the mountains. Jerusalem is 2,500 feet in elevation. The mountains He referred to were mountains on the other side of Jordan, away from the city.

~ Second, He warned that if they were on a housetop, they were not to come down.

~ Third, if they were away from home, they were not to attempt to return to their homes to retrieve personal possessions.

~ Finally, He warned that it would be difficult for a woman with a breast-feeding infant to flee the city. Christ knew what was going to occur in the future.

He knew the Roman soldiers would slaughter everyone within the walls of the city. He knew that if a person returned to his house, hungry mobs would rob him. History reveals a famine so bad that people were killing others for small amounts of food. They were boiling their leather boots and attempting to eat them. Jesus warned that destruction was coming, and He revealed the timing—when Jerusalem was surrounded by armies. He gave a plan of escape—flee to the mountains.

This warning was about 40 years prior to the destruction of Jerusalem and the Temple. About four years before Roman troops seized the holy mountain, a series of signs indicated the soon destruction of the city. These were a combination of supernatural and verbal signs.

Supernatural Signs of the Destruction

According to Jewish historian Josephus (an eyewitness to the destruction of Jerusalem), a star resembling a sword stood over the city. A comet appeared in the sky for a whole year. On the night of the Feast of Unleavened Bread, at the ninth hour, a light appeared in the "holy house" and made it as bright as day (Josephus, *War of the Jews*, Book VI, chapter 5). There was a mixed reaction among those at the Temple:

> *The light seemed to be a good sign to the unskilled, but was so interpreted by the sacred scribes as to portend those events that followed immediately thereafter.*

Josephus continues to describe the unusual phenomena preceding the overthrow of Jerusalem. A heifer (female cow) that was being led into the Temple to be sacrificed gave birth to a lamb. The eastern gate (it took 20 priests to close it) suddenly opened and closed on its own). Once again, there was a split reaction among the people. Josephus recalls:

> *This appeared to the vulgar to be a happy prodigy, as if God did thereby open them the gate of happiness. But the men of learning understood it,*

that the security of their holy house was dissolved of its own accord and that the gate was opened for the advantage of their enemies.

During the Feast of Pentecost, the priests who were ministering heard a voice say, "Let us depart from hence."

Verbal Warnings Before the Invasion

Verbal warnings were given through a husbandman named Jesus of Ananus. Years before the destruction of Jerusalem, he went through the city pronouncing a woe of judgment against the city and the Temple. At the time the city enjoyed peace and prosperity, and his predictions were deemed out of line among the wealthy and the elite. At the Feast of Pentecost he warned:

A voice from the east, a voice from the west, a voice from the four winds, a voice against Jerusalem and against the holy house, a voice against the bridegrooms and the brides, and a voice against the whole people.

Josephus wrote that this stranger cried out day and night in the lanes of the city, pronouncing warnings. Prominent people in the city seized him and beat him, hoping to silence his cries. When he continued his warnings, he was taken into custody by the Roman leaders who had him scourged severely. As he was being whipped he cried, "Woe, woe to Jerusalem."

For seven years he yelled his warnings at every Jewish festival and never lost his voice. When the armies invaded, he was standing on the wall, denouncing the city and announcing judgment on it. Finally he yelled, "Woe unto myself, also!" A stone from a Roman catapult struck him and he died.

Two Opposing Predictions

Two groups had two contrary beliefs. One group recognized the ancient prophecies and the sins of the city, and realized that Jerusalem's days were numbered. Others discovered a sacred oracle in the Temple files that said a leader would be raised up, so they felt Israel was safe. Their faith in this prediction brought a false sense of security, and a belief that nothing bad would happen to the city. Josephus concludes by saying:

But these men interpreted these signals according to their own pleasure; and some of them they utterly despised, until their madness was demonstrated, by both the taking of their city and their own destruction.

These same two groups are present in America. One is a seeker-sensitive, people-pleasing ministry that refuses to preach the Cross, the blood of Christ or the Baptism in the Holy Spirit. They do not believe these things and will not preach them. They mock the idea that God would ever judge America for its sins. The other group discerns the times and knows that Scripture warns them about breaking covenant with God. They recognize the danger of rejecting the truth. A trend of willful disobedience can send divine chastisement on a nation which turns its back on God.

As the Roman 10th Legion broke down the gates of Jerusalem, three types of persons were linked to the destruction.

~   False prophets, encouraging Jews to remain in the walls of the city, saw innocent people slaughtered by the invaders' swords. They had expected a last-minute, divine intervention from God, but it never came because judgment was already set.

~   A second group, resolved to being slaves, simply turned themselves over to the Romans, hoping their lives would be spared. They would simply be displaced from their homes, leaving behind their valuables and personal possessions.

~   The third group was Christians who heeded Jesus' warning to get out of the city and flee to the mountains. Phillip Schaff's *History of the Christian Church* says this group was able to escape during a brief period before the destruction, between A.D. 66 and 70. During this time people had access in and out of the city. Instead of staying around and waiting to see if God would or would not intervene in the situation, they chose to "get out while the getting was good." It was necessary for them to leave familiar surroundings behind, including their homes and property, and relocate in order to escape the judgment on the city. They escaped to Pella, in Jordan, and received asylum. A large Christian community developed from these believers.

When New Orleans was devastated by water, both Christians and non-Christians had to be evacuated and relocated, just as Noah and Lot were permanently removed from their homes and their possessions. Both men were warned to escape prior to the judgment. Believers must learn not to ignore natural and spiritual warning signs.

It is clear that as God warned ancient Jerusalem through numerous signs, both America and the nations of the world are receiving signals from heaven. We who understand the Scriptures are able to discern the times. We must respond accordingly.

America's trouble has been on her coastlines and shores. What is God's message to us during these troubled times?

8

Trouble on America's Coastlines

Thus saith the Lord of hosts, Behold, evil shall go forth from nation to nation, and a great whirlwind shall be raised up from the coasts of the earth (Jeremiah 25:32).

Hurricane and storm surges are nothing new. It has been noted that large destructive hurricanes seem to hit the same areas about every 40 years.

During the 2005 storm season, the most devastating storm to strike America, Hurricane Katrina, hit the Gulf shores of Louisiana, Alabama and Mississippi. It caused damage in the billions of dollars and was the most destructive and costliest natural disaster in the history of the United States.

Three months after the hurricane, the death toll stood at more than 1,400 in seven states: Louisiana, Florida,

Mississippi, Alabama, Georgia, Kentucky and Ohio, with thousands of people still missing and unaccounted for. Emergency workers were finding bodies in New Orleans at the rate of two a day.

After the initial impact, several breaches appeared in the levees protecting New Orleans. The city, which sits below sea level, was suddenly flooded with water from Lake Pontchartrain and the Mississippi River. Thousands were stranded in their homes and apartments, including countless poor people in housing projects.

As the days and weeks passed, the scene turned into something from a horror movie. Commentators described the scenes we watched on television as "hell on earth," as we saw Americans being called refugees for the first time in history.

Having ministered in Louisiana and having minister friends there, I was fully aware that New Orleans had a reputation of being "sin city." It is a fact that in some areas it was not just sin city, but had the nickname of Sodom and Gomorrah.

New Orleans

New Orleans was founded by Jean-Baptise Le Moyne de Bienville as a port colony in 1718. According to its early history, Indians, slaves, thieves, cutthroats, prostitutes and beggars were among the first settlers in the city.

Before the 2005 hurricane hit New Orleans, more than 15 percent of its citizens practiced voodoo. It was introduced through the slave trade around 1510. Voodoo is an ancient African religion which mingled with Catholicism in New Orleans. When the slaves were brought to America, the slave traders tried to separate the slaves from their tribal and pagan beliefs. The slaves simply replaced the names of their African gods with the names of Catholic saints, however, to disguise their religion from the general public.

The island nation of Haiti has the highest concentration of voodoo worship in the western hemisphere, and New Orleans has the second highest level. Before the devastating storm, it was common to see candles and altars in shops, homes and bars across the city. The religion of voodoo has been inbred there for so long, until it became a part of the tradition of the city. The main purpose of voodoo is not only to put a curse on your enemies, but to open yourself up to evil spirits in order to use the power of the evil spirits to get what you want.

Mardi Gras

In mid-February the ancient Romans celebrated *Lupercalia*, a circus-like festival. When Rome embraced Christianity, compromising church fathers felt it was better to incorporate certain aspects of pagan rituals into the new faith than to abolish them. The sad result was that many pagan ideas and concepts were incorporated into the Christian tradition. One of these traditions was Mardi Gras, which is celebrated in New Orleans each February.

I have never participated in or personally witnessed Mardi Gras, but I have friends who would attend in order to witness and minister to the many people present. They all admit it is the most perverse "party" in the United States. The idea for most attendees is to abandon all restraint—including moral restraint—by drinking, partying and having sex before lent arrives. During lent, the person must repent.

This event was celebrated in Paris, France, in the Middle Ages, and was brought to America by the French (a landmark in New Orleans is the French Quarter). Most attendees know about Fat Tuesday, which precedes Ash Wednesday. Some make this a "spiritual" time, but it is actually linked to voodoo. The combination of Mardi Gras and voodoo marked New Orleans as "America's most haunted city" by 1999.

As a historical footnote, Haiti was once under French control. Centuries ago, the Haitian leaders offered their island to Satan if he would help free them from France's control. As the French gave up control, Satan took the island.

Today, the cities in Haiti are known as some of the poorest in the Western Hemisphere. Superstition and poverty reign throughout the island, except in areas where there is a strong Christian presence.

Nations whose religion centers around idolatry, ancestor and spirit worship are nations ruined by poverty. Spirits operating through religions such as voodoo bring a curse of oppression on the people and their lands.

Sins of the Cities

New Orleans has been noted for many years as "sin city," and a place to get drunk and party. The seven main sins that infected New Orleans and other cities are:

1. Prostitution
2. Homosexuality/Cross-dressing
3. Strip clubs
4. Voodoo worship
5. Illegal Drugs
6. Alcoholism and drunkenness
7. Occultism

Ezekiel lists the sins of Sodom before God's judgment:

Behold, this was the iniquity of thy sister Sodom, pride, fulness of bread, and abundance of idleness was in her and in her daughters, neither did she strengthen the hand of the poor and needy. And they were haughty, and committed abomination before me: therefore I took them away as I saw good (Ezekiel 16:49, 50).

The six sins listed by the prophet were:

~ Overabundance of food

~ Prosperous ease (idleness)

~ Idleness among the young women (laziness)

~ Not helping the poor

~ Haughty (arrogance)

~ Committing abominations (homosexuality)

No one who understands the Scripture would doubt that the destruction of Sodom was some form of divine chastisement or judgment. What about a major city in America, however?

Was It Divine Chastisement?

The most difficult question to answer is, *Was such a tragic event possibly a time of divine chastisement for the sins of the cities?* The answer is controversial, due to the fact that so many good people suffered loss and pain. Before attempting to answer this question, we should look at the Biblical definition of the word "judgment."

The Old Testament Word for "judgment" is the Hebrew word *mishpat*, which means to pass a verdict, whether favorable or unfavorable. It alludes to God passing a final sentence on someone or something.

1. In the New Testament, several different words are used for the word "judgment." The word *praetorium* is used for "judgment hall" where Jesus stood trial (John 18:28).

2. There is also a heavenly judgment where believers will stand before God and be judged for their actions on earth: "For we must all appear before the judgment seat of Christ" (2 Corinthians 5:10). This is called the *Bema* seat of Christ (Romans 14:10-14). According to Thayer, the judgment seat or *bema* was "a raised place mounted by steps; a platform used as the official seat of a judge." When Paul uses judgment in Philippians 1:9, he is alluding to correctly discerning a matter.

3. Another word in 1 Corinthians 7:25 means an opinion based on information in a court. Only one *krima*, alludes to making a decision related to a crime.

4. One of the primary words for judgment is the word *krisis*. From this word we derive the English word "crisis." This word means a separating, and then a decision. It is used in a forensic sense and especially of divine judgment.

To summarize: when God sends judgment the crisis causes a separation in which individuals make a decision to either repent and follow God or to continue to reject God. The Almighty permits severe trouble, or a crisis, after He has investigated the situation and believes the object therein needs to be judged.

How Does Judgment Happen?

Throughout the Scriptures four main instruments are used to initiate judgment:

~ The sword (war)

~ Fire (burning cities)

~ Famine (drought, natural disasters, floods)

~ Pestilence (plague and disease)

The Bigger Question

All believers understand why God would permit divine chastisement or a judgment on a wicked city such as Sodom and Gomorrah—or a contemporary city whose sins have reached the heavens. It is difficult, however, for some to believe God would permit the homes and businesses of Christians to be lost along with the homes of voodoo worshipers, drug dealers and porno kings.

God often gives warnings to provide a way of escape before a major incident occurs. This warning can come through His Word, a dream, a vision, a sign or a prophetic alert. It can also be given through warnings in the news media. In the Scripture, warnings are often given to escape to the mountains.

When the five kings of the plain fought against the kings of Shinar, some fell into the slime pits near the Dead Sea and others escaped into the surrounding mountains:

> *And the vale of Siddim was full of slimepits; and the kings of Sodom and Gomorrah fled, and fell there; and they that remained fled to the mountain* (Genesis 14:10).

Later, angels warned Lot that all five cities of the plain would be destroyed by God's wrath. One small city was nestled on a mountain overlooking the other four larger cities. Lot requested to flee to the Zoar, the small city on the mountain. The angels said:

And when they had brought them forth, they said, Escape for your life! Do not look behind you or stop anywhere in the whole valley; escape to the mountains [of Moab], lest you be consumed (Genesis 19:17, *AMP*).

Lot lost everything, but his life was spared. Jesus told His followers to leave Jerusalem and head for the mountains (Matthew 24:16). During the dreaded Tribulation, men will take to the mountains:

And the kings of the earth, and the great men, and the rich men, and the chief captains, and the mighty men, and every bondman, and every free man, hid themselves in the dens and in the rocks of the mountains (Revelation 6:15).

The prophet Ezekiel speaks of judgment coming and how some escaped to the mountains:

The sword is without, and the pestilence and the famine within: he that is in the field shall die with the sword; and he that is in the city, famine and pestilence shall devour him. But they that escape of them shall escape, and shall be on the mountains like doves of the valleys, all of them mourning, every one for his iniquity (Ezekiel 7:15, 16).

Going to the Mountains

Instead of making a direct statement, often a verse implies a truth hidden within the passage. In each reference it mentions fleeing to the mountains for protection and fleeing from trouble. Jesus said that trouble would occur on the sea and the waves. If storms are increasing in intensity and in number, then the coastal areas will be the strongest hit. Do these verses indicate that there will be more safety in the mountains than in other areas?

Clearly, the coastal areas of the world are experiencing a shaking of the seas. The Pacific Rim saw a deadly Tsunami, killing over 200,000 in 11 nations along the coastal areas. India experienced monsoons, and the Philippines, floods. In 2004, Florida experienced four large hurricanes, and three different southern states saw entire communities wiped out.

A hurricane and a tornado take on the form of a whirlwind or a twister. The Biblical prophet Jeremiah saw a vision of how whirlwinds would bring death and destruction through the earth:

Thus says the Lord of hosts: "Behold, disaster shall go forth from nation to nation, and a great whirlwind shall be raised up from the farthest parts of the earth. And at that day the slain of the Lord shall be from one end of the earth even to the other end of the earth. They shall not be lamented, or gathered, or buried; they shall become refuse on the ground (Jeremiah 25:32, 33).

Behold, the whirlwind of the Lord goeth forth with fury, a continuing whirlwind: it shall fall with pain upon the head of the wicked. The fierce anger of the Lord shall not return, until he hath done it, and until he has performed the intents of his heart: in the latter days ye shall consider it (Jeremiah 30:23, 24).

What About the Righteous?

Lot and his family moved into the city of Sodom, not knowing that the wickedness of the city was gaining the attention of

God. Once the iniquity was full, God sent two angels to warn Lot and provide a way of escape. Lot was a righteous man. This is alluded to by the apostle Peter in 2 Peter 2:4-10:

> *If God did not spare the angels who sinned, but cast them down to hell and delivered them into chains of darkness, to be reserved for judgment; and did not spare the ancient world, but saved Noah, one of eight people, a preacher of righteousness, bringing in the flood on the world of the ungodly;*
>
> *and turning the cities of Sodom and Gomorrah into ashes, condemned them to destruction, making them an example to those who afterward would live ungodly; and delivered righteous Lot, who was oppressed by the filthy conduct of the wicked (for that righteous man, dwelling among them, tormented his righteous soul from day to day by seeing and hearing their lawless deeds)—*
>
> *then the Lord knows how to deliver the godly out of temptations and to reserve the unjust under punishment for the day of judgment, and especially those who walk according to the flesh in the lust of uncleanness and despise authority. They are presumptuous, self-willed.*

Many scholars believe 10 family members were connected to Lot when he lived in Sodom. These included several sons-in-law and daughters (Genesis 19:14). However, only Lot, his wife and two daughters escaped. Lot left his home, his furniture, his clothing, his food and personal possessions. He escaped with the clothes on his back, and lived in a cave for a period of time, just as many Christians have had to live in temporary quarters after God's selective reproof destroyed an area.

Lot was called a "righteous man" by Peter. Although he lost everything, his life was spared. He and his two daughters eventually moved out of the cave and had to rebuild. Often those who survive a disaster will say that what they lost can be replaced but their family is the most important gift they have. Thankfully, Lot heeded God's warning.

Selective Judgment

Several years ago the Holy Spirit impressed me that we would soon enter a time of selective blessings and selective judgment. The coming moves of the Holy Spirit would not sweep the entire nation as a blanket, but would fall on selected areas where saints have been in prayer and deep intercession for revival. Likewise, judgment (divine chastisement) would come in selected areas. The example is Lot and Zoar. This small community was a part of the five cities marked for destruction; however, Zoar was spared because Lot needed a place of protection and security.

The Separation

In these final days there will be a spiritual separation of the wheat from the tares and the sheep from the goats—the righteous from the unrighteous. The separation principle is clear in the Book of Exodus where God is sending judgment to the Egyptians. The Hebrews lived in the same geographical region where the plagues were striking the Egyptians; yet, God made a difference between the two. The Almighty said:

> *I will make a difference between My people and your people. Tomorrow this sign shall be* (Exodus 8:23).

When the judgment of the flies arrived, the Egyptians were beating them away . . . but the Hebrews saw none!

> *In that day I will set apart the land of Goshen, in which My people dwell, that no swarms of flies shall be there, in order that you may know that I am the Lord in the midst of the land* (Exodus 8:22).

The plague of darkness should have affected both the Hebrews and Egyptians; God, however, had provided light for His people:

> *They did not see one another; nor did anyone rise from his place for three days. But all the children of Israel had light in their dwellings* (Exodus 10:23).

Moses warned that a plague of deadly hail was coming to the area. He instructed the Hebrews to house their cattle in their homes for protection from the hailstorm. Some in Egypt ignored the warning. Guess whose cows survived when *hail* broke out?

> *But he who did not regard the word of the Lord left his servants and his livestock in the field* (Exodus 9:21).

The mercy of God upon His chosen people was so great that no hail fell in the land of Goshen, a place marked for the Jewish people:

> *Only in the land of Goshen, where the children of Israel were, there was no hail* (Exodus 9:26).

We must remember that in some cities it has been the sins of the people that have brought certain income-producing business into the region. This includes drugs, alcohol, pornography, prostitution, large block parties with profane and vulgar interaction, gay parades and other fleshly sins.

A city built on honest business and the integrity of honest leadership will be blessed in many ways. Sin cities may prosper for a season, but that season will be short lived when God performs His personal investigation.

Th℮ Final Sins of th℮ Fath℮rs

Prophetic Scripture indicates that the gay lifestyle will be one of the prominent sins during the time of the end. Jesus compared the seasons of his return to the days of Lot (Luke 17:28). This righteous man was living in a large city in which the young and old men were involved in homosexual activity (Genesis 19:4, 5). This same sin will infest the major cities of the world prior to Christ's coming.

The city of Jerusalem will be called spiritually Egypt and Sodom during its final days (Revelation 11:8). Even the future Antichrist will be a person who will have no desire for women (Daniel 11:37). While many Americans no longer consider same-sex relations as wrong, the Bible gives this warning using the example of the destruction of Sodom:

Turning the cities of Sodom and Gomorrah into ashes, [God] condemned them to destruction, making them an example to those who afterward would live ungodly (2 Peter 2:6).

Sodom and Gomorrah, and the cities around them in a similar manner to these, having given themselves over to sexual immorality and gone after strange flesh, are set forth as an example, suffering the vengeance of eternal fire (Jude 7).

The New Testament writers warn future generations not to follow the same sins of Sodom, since the fiery judgment against the city is an example of the same type of judgment that will follow the same types of sins.

Once again, it is up to intercessors to stand in the gap and pray for the nations, calling individuals to humility and repentance. I have met numerous people who were in a backslidden condition and who came back to God as a result of personal losses caused by the storms. Their spiritual condition was far more important to God than their economic portfolios.

We can all rebuild from a personal loss, but can never gain back a lost soul once it steps into eternity. This is why the church must unite in prayer and preaching the truth to break the spirits attempting to control those living in our nation.

In our next chapter, I will share with you the strongest spirit that is controlling America, and needs to be broken—the spirit of *pharmakia.*

9

Breaking America's Pharmakia Prince Spirit

If every nation on earth has a leading national bondage, what is the spirit of bondage over America? From chapters 4 through 22, the vision of John recorded in the Book of Revelation is a vision concerning "things to come" (Revelation 1:8). The apocalyptic Book reveals numerous truths about the time of the end, including the major sins that will infect the nations during the time of the Great Tribulation.

> *But the rest of mankind, who were not killed by these plagues, did not repent of the works of their hands, that they should not worship demons, and idols of gold, silver, brass, stone, and wood, which can neither see nor hear nor walk. And they did not repent of their murders or their sorceries or their sexual immorality or their thefts* (Revelation 9:20, 21).

Four end-time sins are:

~ Idol worship

~ Sexual Immorality

~ Killing other people

~ Sorceries

Nations of Asia, like India, are steeped in idol worship. Sexual immorality is considered a normal human desire and function in all Gentile nations. Murder in the guise of abortion is an acceptable form of birth control. But what does the word *sorceries* mean, and what controls this sin?

The Prince Spirits

Both angels and strong evil prince spirits are given authority over nations on earth. The archangel Michael is called the "chief prince" for the nation of Israel (Daniel 10:13;21; 12:1). The Hebrew word for chief is *ri-shown* and alludes to an angel first in time, place or rank. The word prince is *sar* in Hebrew, and means a captain or a general. Michael was one of the chief angels of God's creation.

Michael's involvement with Israel is so important that centuries ago he personally wrestled with Satan concerning the physical body of Moses (Jude 9). Michael also has a host of angels under his command, and they will remove Satan and his angels from the second heaven and cast them to the earth at the high point of the seven-year Tribulation (Revelation 12:7, 8).

Satan also has an entourage of evil spirits, identified with the title *principalities* (Ephesians 6:12). These strong spirits are demonic generals, and are under Satan's direct control. They are involved in the affairs of nations, especially nations linked to prophetic seasons. These spirits are mentioned in

Daniel 10. Daniel was fasting for 21 days to receive the understanding to a vision he had received.

An angel of God appeared to him after the three weeks, and informed the prophet that his message was hindered by a prince of the Kingdom of Persia. This Persian spirit restrained the messenger of God in the second heaven, leaving Daniel to intercede his way alone into a breakthrough.

At the time of this heavenly battle, the Jews had returned to Jerusalem and were rebuilding the Temple. At the same time, they were being greatly hindered by Satan himself (see Zechariah 3:1-3). Evil "prince" spirits were assigned to hinder and delay the prophetic progress of the Jews and the destiny of God's chosen.

In the New Testament the word *principalities* is also used of earthly magistrates and governmental leaders. I have said that "principalities work through personalities." No evil spirits can work in a community, city or a nation, without a willing vessel submitting to the evil thoughts being shot like darts into their minds from these agents of evil.

Both angels of God and spirits in Satan's kingdom have been active in the heavens and on the earth since the fall of man in the Garden of Eden. As men moved throughout the earth setting up cities and empires, both angels and prince spirits took their domain in and around these important centers of human activity.

Selecting the Strongholds

How does a particular prince spirit of Satan determine what region of earth to seize? I believe the sins of the early founders often become a spiritual magnet to attract spirits to a particular sin. For example, some of them are:

~ Lying spirits (2 Chronicles 18:21)

~ Seducing spirits (1 Timothy 4:1)

~ Unclean spirits (Matthew 12:43)

~ Foul spirits (Mark 9:25)

~ Deaf and dumb spirits (Mark 9:25)

~ Spirits of infirmity (Luke 13:12)

~ Spirits of divination (Acts 16:16)

~ Spirits of slumber (Romans 11:8)

~ Hindering spirits (2 Corinthians 12:7)

Each spirit has a particular feature that attracts it to the particular sickness, problem, circumstance, and so forth. After the fall of Adam there were righteous men who called on the name of the Lord (Genesis 4:26). Enoch was so close to God he was translated, and Noah found enough grace in God's eyes to be protected from the flood (Genesis 5:24; 6:8). There were, however, many wicked men whose imaginations were continually evil and who promoted violence (Genesis 6:13).

Between the days of Adam and Noah's flood is 1,658 years. During this time a strange race of giants was conceived on earth. They were the offspring of fallen angels and the daughters of men (See our video, *The Mystery of Giants*). After the flood of Noah, according to Jewish belief, the spirits of the giants became the evil spirits, roaming the earth attacking men.

After the flood the three sons of Noah—Shem, Ham and Japheth—settled with their families into three regions around the Mediterranean. As the population increased, so did the iniquity. Soon the spirits of evil were roaming the earth, seeing who they could control. Thus, idolatry, witchcraft, sorcery and other evils began to spread throughout the earth. Eventually, strong spirits marked their territory for long-term dominion.

Spirits are Territorial

In Mark 5, Christ ministered in the land of the Gadarenes, a region of mountains east of the Sea of Galilee. A madman who was possessed by thousands of evil spirits met Him there. The main demon was named Legion, a Latin word referring to 6,000 Roman soldiers. The spirits begged Christ "earnestly that He would not send them out of the country" (Mark 5:10).

Christ commanded the demons to depart from the man, and the spirits that exited the madman entered 2,000 swine that were feeding on the hillside. These particular spirits wanted to remain in the region with which they were familiar. This was due, perhaps, to a large Temple constructed for the Greek idol, Zeus, which towered over the lake. The priest of Zeus offered pigs on the altar! These spirits entered the pigs who were being raised for the altar of Zeus. Jesus not only delivered the maniac from the evil spirits, but He ruined Zeus' offerings!

This incident reveals that spirits seek to remain in the land where they have organized and settled. The Prince of Persia controlled the land of Persia, just as the Price of Greece had his grip on Greece (Daniel 10:20).

How Spirits Take Dominion of an Area

Every major city has a "personality." Some have an oppressive atmosphere and others have a seducing attraction. I have spent the night in hotels and had difficulty sleeping because I could sense strong spiritual opposition and activity in the heavens. I believe the spirits influencing the leaders in any city are spirits that occupied that area as the land was being settled.

Before the Pilgrims founded our first colonies, there were numerous Indian tribes scattered throughout this continent. These included the Delaware, Iroquois, Cherokee, Choctaw, Cheyenne, Navaho, Creek, Seminole and Chickasaw, to name a few. Most Indian tribes had a medicine man. This person was a spiritual-religious leader, not a medical doctor.

In such states as New Mexico, there are Shamans. These powerful men are controlled by evil spirits and can perform supernatural feats that frighten and impress followers. Included in their occult arsenal are objects called *dream catchers* and *Kachina Dolls*. The dolls are stylized religious icons, meticulously carved from cottonwood root and painted to represent figures of native American mythology.

Missionaries have informed me that the Shamans curse the dolls and sell them to the white man in order to curse them for oppressing the Indians.

There are also *skin walkers* who can levitate and have the power to curse people with sickness and accidents. Skin walkers are feared by some Indians and revered by others. These occult leaders use various drugs to enhance their spiritual perception. One of the tragedies in the Indian tribes is alcoholism. Much of this can be traced back to the white man, who gave hard liquor to the ancestors of the Indians when they were trading, buying and selling.

In the early days of the colonies, there were strange manifestations from areas such as Massachusetts. In the Salem area, numerous people were accused of being possessed with demons. These individuals were accused of being witches and were burned at the stake. Several centuries have passed; yet today, Salem, Massachusetts, is a stronghold for rampant witchcraft and the practice of the occult.

Another example is the state of California. This large western state became famous when gold was found at Sutter's Mill near San Francisco in 1849. This discovery initiated a massive exodus from east to west, as miners and common men sought wealth through the lure of gold.

The rough journey to the west was often made by men as women and children stayed hundreds of miles away, keeping the home fires burning. On Saturday nights, men would often dress up as women and the other miners would dance with them, since "real" women were not in the mining camps. This led, at times, to other activities; some of these activities included same-sex relations.

Today, the state seal of California depicts Minerva, a Roman goddess—a female—dressed in a Roman soldier's military outfit. She is overlooking the San Francisco Bay! For years, the city of San Francisco has been recognized as the gay capital of America and as one of America's most liberal cities. How strange that this woman dressed like a man overlooks the bay.

Some of America's cities were founded by leaders who were heavily involved in secret orders and mystical lodges. This secrecy eventually led to a spirit that hid the many sins and iniquities of its leaders and opened the door to corruption.

America's Prince Spirit

Individual cities have their own personalities and all 50 states have their own chief spirits working within the borders of that state. America, however, is a nation with 50 states and one capital, Washington. D.C. Is there one main principality hovering over our nation? If so, what is its name and assignment?

I believe America's chief evil spirit is linked to the main sin that is sweeping our nation. It is the sin of sorcery.

> *And they did not repent of their murders or their sorceries or their sexual immorality or their thefts* (Revelation 9:21).

The English word "sorcery" paints a mental picture of a sorcerer or a witch casting spells on its victims. The Greek word, however, carries a broader meaning. The word "sorceries" in Revelation 9:21 is *pharmakia*. We derive the words "pharmacy" and "pharmaceutical" from a form of this word. The Greek dictionary gives these comments concerning the word *pharmakia*:

> *Signifying 'devoted to magical arts,' is used as a noun, a sorcerer, especially one who uses drugs, potions, spells and enchantments* (W. E. Vines, *Dictionary of New Testament Words*).

The word can signify the use of drugs. May I say this is the root cause for most crimes in America, the use of illegal drugs?

The vast majority of men and women incarcerated in American prisons are there because of selling or buying hardcore drugs. The majority of crimes committed, such as robbery, break-ins and even murder, are a result of stealing money or stealing something to sell for money to support a drug habit and drug addiction. America is an addicted society.

In the early church the Christians encountered the spirit of sorcery, in different forms. During the revival at Ephesus, thousands of dollars of occult books were burned (Acts 19). In Samaria, Simon the sorcerer bewitched the people and was rebuked by Peter during the great Samaritan revival (Acts 8). In Paphos, Elymas the sorcerer was a main leader (Acts 13).

In Phillipi, Paul encountered a woman with a spirit of divination. The word divination is the word *puthon*, or in English, python. There was a large temple with a snake. The people would go to the snake to receive information about their future. Once this evil spirit was cast out of this female fortuneteller, the men of the city became angry at Paul because the superstitious citizens refused to buy their idols.

During the 1990's television was filled with info-mercials of so-called psychics who claimed to tell your future for only $5.95 a minute. Ignorant Americans ran up large phone bills to hear an alleged psychic tell them things they already knew! One woman admitted to spending $30,000 over a few months because she was addicted to talking to the psychic. She wouldn't go out of the house without consulting the so-called fortuneteller. These money-making psychics failed to handle their debts and all of them went off the air, unable to pay the high cost of television air time.

These fakers were not the real spirits in the nation. The real spirits were killing and destroying the minds of millions of Americans through drug addiction. The *pharmakia* spirit, a spirit of sorcery, is the chief spirit controlling the United States. Millions have experimented with and are addicted to:

~ Marijuana, better known as pot or weed

~ LSD

~ Heroin

~ Cocaine

~ Crack Cocaine

~ Methamphetamine, better known as meth

One of the most addictive drugs is cocaine. For years I thought cocaine was a modern invention. I was shocked to discover how long this drug has been in our culture. This information I am reporting was published in the May, 1984 issue of *Life* magazine.

Cocaine was first introduced in the 1880s. It was derived from the coca plant and was crushed into powder and introduced as medical relief from sinus headaches and hysteria. By 1886, the *New York Herald* wrote that the "whole town has gone mad for cocaine." Five years later a coca wine was introduced that existed for 23 years. It received praise from three popes, 16 heads of state and 8,000 doctors. From 1898 to 1902, cocaine imports rose 40 percent, while the population grew only 10 percent.

Perhaps the most interesting early link was with a drink concoction developed by John Pemberton. The pharmacist wanted to invent a "pick-me-up" drink, so he prepared a special syrup he mixed with soda fountain water. One of the key ingredients in the early drink was cocaine. The new drink would be called Coca Cola! The drink became a smash hit, even though the cocaine was removed in 1903 after a presidential commission revealed the danger and addictive power of cocaine.

Some of the early black-and-white silent films showed movie stars using "nose powders, by snorting them," followed by printed signs to show the dangers of the drug. From the 1930s to the 1950s, cocaine use dropped, but was resurrected during the 1960s through the hippie movement and the rock music industry. The drug received a boost from the movie *Easy Rider*.

The Addiction Demon

Millions of Americans are addicted to something. For some, it is illegal drugs; and for others, pornography. Some cannot break the desire to gamble and some are bound by alcohol. The statistics on alcohol in America are staggering:

~ 150 million people drink alcohol in America.

~ 21 million people are alcoholics.

~ 14 million alcoholics are employed in the work force.

~ 25 percent of American families are directly affected by alcohol.

~ 18 percent use marijuana at least monthly.

~ 8 percent (almost 1 in 10) use cocaine at least once a month.

~ 75 percent of all drug users are white.

~ 70 percent are employed.

~ 89 percent are 18 years old or older.

Cursed Cities

The spirit of drug addiction has brought a terrible curse on our cities. This spirit breeds off of a spirit of poverty. The largest drug strongholds are among the poor in the inner cities. The feeling of hopelessness hovering over the projects induces a desire to escape the pain, suffering, loneliness and rejection of life. Drugs become the addicts' best friend, taking them to high highs and low lows, promising them a trip of escape that ends in a pit of more despair.

Poor young men join gangs for acceptance and survival. They begin selling drugs to their own friends so they can get a small piece of the pie. Soon the children are seeing "Junior" with gold chains hanging half-way down his chest, driving a new car. Sadly, they don't see Junior in the morgue 12 months later, or attend Junior's trial for selling the illegal powder.

A former big-time drug dealer told me that the little man means nothing to the big bosses. They are expendable, and are knocked off on a continual basis. He also said the reason America cannot get a grip on illegal drugs is because too many men in high places are paid to turn their heads the other way. This includes certain members of the border police, U.S. Customs, and local police. He also said that the payoffs go as high as to reach the men in Washington. He said:

> Often, when you see a drug bust, it is a bad batch that is permitted to be seized for the news—so it will appear the war on drugs is being won. All the time the real good "stuff" is coming from another direction. The war on drugs will never be won because too many men have their hand in the pockets of the drug kingpins.

Drug money from Afghanistan helps provide funds for terrorists, and drug money from Lebanon was also used to provide weapons for terror groups. Yes, America has been hypnotized by greed and addiction. Sadly, this addiction is being passed from generation to generation. This is the reason that this spirit works so diligently. The attack is always about the future "seed."

Every sin in our generation is an assignment against children. Abortion stops the life of a human soul. Same-sex couples cannot reproduce a child. Drugs can make a man impotent, and alcohol destroys the family unit. The AIDS virus destroys the future of an entire generation. The Enemy's attack on the "seed" is seen in more child abuse, molestation and the rise of pedophiles.

What Can We Do?

It is not wise for a believer to challenge head-on the ruling spirits over a nation or a country. There is evidence that those who have attempted this have often found themselves fighting life-and-death personal battles that overwhelmed their souls. In the Bible, God sent His highest ranking angels to directly engage in spiritual conflict with the Prince Spirits. In Daniel 10, Michael the archangel had to come to the rescue of Gabriel who was hindered by the Prince of Persia for 21 days.

We have been given spiritual authority through prayer, however! As an example, Cali, Columbia is noted as the drug capital of the world. Years ago I was the speaker for a telethon in Clearwater, Florida. The station owner, Bob D'Andrea was led of the Lord to help place a stronger television tower in Cali, Columbia, so the gospel could reach more in the city. That night we raised $90,000. Bob called the main pastor of the area, Jose, and awoke him to tell him the money was raised for the tower.

On live television, Jose began to tell us that he and his associate pastor had received a death threat from the drug lords of Columbia. The pastor had started a prayer meeting, asking God to bring down the drug kingpins in the nation.

At first, people were afraid to attend the meeting since the drug cartel was known to kill people with whom they disagreed. Soon the crowds swelled to over 30,000. As prayer went up, the drugs lords went down. One at a time, they were either captured or killed. In fact, nine of the 10 were removed by the power of prayer!

Just as Michael the archangel restrained the Prince of Persia, we need to ask God to send His strongest heavenly, warring angels to engage the battle in the heavens over America. We need the spirit of *pharmakia* restrained and his authority broken, so that the generation coming up will have no interest in drugs, alcohol and the bondages that come with addictions. If it can happen in Columbia, it can happen in America. God is looking for the intercessors.

So I sought for a man among them who would make a wall, and stand in the gap before Me on behalf of the land, that I should not destroy it; but I found no one (Ezekiel 22:30).

With Christ, You Can Break the Addiction in Your Life

Sadly, some have already fallen victim to the prince spirits that are warring against America. If you are addicted to a *pharmakia* spirit or some type of drug is ruining your life, you can be delivered through the power of God. King Jesus has power over every prince spirit, and over all the power of the devil and his kingdom. If you want to be delivered from an addiction, here are some positive steps to deliverance:

Step One: Admit you cannot conquer your addiction alone.

If you could overcome it in yourself, you would already be free. The first thing you have to do is admit your own helplessness. Confess that you are unable to get a grip on whatever you are addicted to. Admit that this addiction is controlling your life. You find it impossible to quit. You cannot resist, and you are no longer in control of your life.

Step Two: Accept the fact that only God can break the addiction and get you out of this stifling, suffocating situation.

After trying to break away so many times and failing every time you tried, you have to come to realize that only God can help you out of this situation. You may have admitted this to yourself before, but you are convinced of it now more than ever. Accept the reality that only God can deliver you.

Step Three: Determine to put your total and complete trust in God.

Realize that both life and death are in God's hands. He can save our souls and deliver us from evil, but He can also control every aspect of our existence. It is only logical that we bring this problem to Him and seek His help first and foremost.

Step Four: Confess your addiction(s) to God.

Repent sincerely and honestly to Him, specifically naming your addiction(s). It is also good to confess to another—someone you trust and whom you believe cares for you and has your best interests in mind. This person will make covenant with you and help you overcome the Enemy. Believe that God will forgive you of your sins and will heal you of your addictions.

Step Five: Believe that God has answered your prayer and delivered you from the chains of addiction.

Sincere repentance must be followed by action, however. Be ready to do whatever is necessary to change, no matter how difficult or painful. For example, if you are addicted to alcohol, don't go near a bar or anywhere you would be tempted to drink. If you are addicted to pornography, quit surfing the Internet, looking for pornography. Avoid whatever tempts you even if you have to run, just as Joseph did in Egypt (Genesis 39:12).

Step Six: Develop a close relationship with God.

Pray regularly. Read God's Word. Learn to live in the Word. This gives you unbelievable spiritual strength and faith. It develops confidence in you and gives you spiritual muscle.

As we battle for the souls of our families, we are also battling for the soul of America, as we will expose in the next chapter

10

American Enemies of Religious Freedom

A merica has many enemies. Osama bin Laden declared war on America in the name of the al-Qaida network. He and his allies boast of an Islamic Jihad against America and the West. Blatant terrorism and many other enemies of this country and of the American people exist in a frightful way.

The greatest enemy of religious freedom, however, is not Osama bin Laden or communism or others you may mention. The enemies within America are more sinister and threatening because they deal in deceit and attack us where we are most vulnerable. Perhaps the greatest enemy to religious freedom in America today is an organization with the innocuous name of the American Civil Liberties Union, or the ACLU. The organization's official web page says its purpose is noble and virtuous. This is what it says:

The ACLU is our nation's guardian of liberty. We work daily . . . to defend and preserve the individual rights and liberties guaranteed to every person in this country by the Constitution and laws of the United States. Our job is to conserve America's original civic values—the Constitution and the Bill of Rights.

Reality contradicts that statement of purpose. Despite its rhetoric about defending the Constitution, democracy and the right to choose, the ACLU has demonstrated that the opposite is true. Repeatedly, they have waged war on the rights of free Americans to choose and/or to be heard.

For example, when voters have a chance to vote on a law or constitutional amendment defining marriage as one man and one woman, the ACLU brings a suit in a federal court to try to muzzle the people and stop the vote. They want the courts to redefine marriage. They wish to create a new meaning for *family* and establish countless new rights that cannot be found in the Constitution.

The ACLU and groups like them cloak themselves in language about defending rights and freedom, but they openly brush aside their noble ideals and opt to illegitimately use the judiciary and the courts to attain goals they cannot accomplish at the ballot box.

Their actions reveal a primary philosophy: *the ends justify the means.* To them, their cause is too important to be left to the American people, so they work diligently to impose their vision for America on the vast majority who do not share that vision.

The unfolding agenda of the ACLU is revealing. While claiming to protect the rights of all Americans, this organization intentionally overprotects some rights, ignoring other rights our Founding Fathers intended to protect. The ACLU's goals are more than just political; they seek to actually snuff out freedom of Christian expression in the public marketplace. Ultimately, they want a secular-humanistic state based on evolving values and human reason. They want a country that has no regard for God's authority at the center of government.

History of the ACLU

One of the great myths of the 21st century is the belief that the ACLU is an organization that had a noble beginning but has somehow strayed off course. That myth is untrue. The founders and organization set a course to destroy America's religious freedom and Christian values from the start.

In its beginning, the ACLU had strong socialist and communist ties. As early as 1931, the U.S. Congress was alarmed by the ACLU's devotion to communism. A report by the Special House Committee to Investigate Communist Activities stated:

> *The American Civil Liberties Union is closely affiliated with the communist movement in the United States, and fully 90 percent of its efforts are on behalf of communists who have come into conflict with the law. It claims to stand for free speech, free press and free assembly, but it is quite apparent that the main function of the ACLU is an attempt to protect the communists.*

Roger Baldwin and Crystal Eastman founded the ACLU in 1920, and dedicated it from the beginning to leftist causes. The histories of these two individuals contradict their claims of patriotism and respect for the Constitution, and speak volumes about the ACLU's true goals. From the start they considered the Bill of Rights "nothing but a parchment barrier to the misdeeds of the government." Most of the founders were unprincipled socialists, social activists, communists and sympathizers.

Among the first board members were Elizabeth Gurley Flynn, an infamous American communist who was given a state funeral in Red Square in 1964; William Z. Foster, once a Communist Party presidential candidate; Earl Browder, general secretary of the Communist Party of the United States; and Norman Thomas, probably America's most famous socialist.

Browder admitted that the ACLU served as a "transmission belt" for the party. Baldwin agreed, claiming, "I don't regret being a part of the communist tactic which increased the effectiveness of a good cause." In fact, he openly sought the complete destruction of American society. Fifteen years after the founding of the ACLU, he wrote:

> *I am for Socialism, disarmament and, ultimately, for the abolishing of the State itself. I seek the social ownership of property, the abolition of the propertied class and sole control of those who produce wealth. Communism is the goal.*

The ACLU Today

Current leaders of the ACLU reason away morality by saying that values change, depending on circumstances and motivation. They deny the very spirit of our unique American, Judeo-Christian-based government.

Our founders purposely based our government on divine design in order to create and ensure order. Laws were to come from the people as they exercised their God-given right to self-rule. These laws, by definition, would be respectful of God and the godly principles of government articulated in the Declaration of Independence.

The Founders understood that as people walk with God, their values will be based on His universal values. Godly values are correct anyplace, anytime—past, present and future—and under any circumstances.

The ACLU's evolutionary view of values is diametrically opposed to the Founders' view of eternal values. The ACLU wants human reason to be the god of this nation because without God's true, universal values at the foundation of our government, the courts and the media could replace them with court-justified values. Calling humans mere accidents of nature with values that change over time, the ACLU seeks to deprive Americans of the right to express their heritage of purpose and destiny. They do this by seeking to forbid the teaching of anything different from their own slanted views.

In public schools, God's universal values are rapidly being replaced with situational ethics. A gospel of tolerance is preached to justify immorality. For example, when Christian students, in classroom discussions, take a stand for absolute right and wrong behaviors, they are accused of being intolerant and held up to ridicule.

This process has grown over the past few years until it has slowly poisoned the social mindset of even Christians in America. Since tolerance has been taught as the supreme value, even some Christians have been duped or intimidated into feeling they cannot take a stand against immoral laws, even though they personally honor God.

A logical result of the humanistic-atheistic state is the eradication of the Ten Commandments from public places. Ironically, these principles, actually God's Law, makes people aware of sin, and people don't want to repent of sin. Current trends feature courts accepting the arguments of fast-talking lawyers who call sin a disease and argue that their clients should escape the consequences of their actions. A lawyer will argue in court that a drunk driver should not go to jail for manslaughter after killing a family in a car crash because he suffers from the "disease" of alcoholism.

Because people haven't learned that it is their responsibility to stand up for godly principles at the foundation of our government, some—even some Christians—think homosexual marriage should be legal.

Founding Documents of the Founding Fathers

In Genesis 22:18, God promised Abraham, "In your seed all the nations of the earth shall be blessed, because you have obeyed My voice." The eternal principle is: Obedience to God brings blessings! Not only personal blessings, but when we obey God He uses us to bless others. This is true for nations as well as individuals. How do we know?

In Galatians 3:8, Paul quoted this same scripture and made a spiritual application that includes us today:

> *And the Scripture, foreseeing that God would justify the Gentiles by faith, preached the gospel to Abraham beforehand, saying, "In you all the nations shall be blessed. . . . that the blessing of Abraham might come upon the Gentiles in Christ Jesus, that we might receive the promise of the Spirit through faith.*

America, too, has blessed the nations because we have been obedient to God. The Founding Fathers never wanted tyrants, within or without, to lead our nation. They never believed in the rule of a few elite over the majority. They never intended for fast-talking lawyers, in collusion with agreeable judges, to run the United States of America.

So they worded the Declaration of Independence to clearly reject any government by tyrants who would use armies, armadas or attorneys to force laws on the people.

Apologists for the ACLU will tell you that the organization was started to protect the Bill of Rights. Its activists felt that the government had too much freedom and power to oppress individual rights, so they began to sympathize with various peoples and groups. So they began defending the racially segregated, some who experienced sexual discrimination and workers who wanted to meet together to start trade unions.

Then they expanded their mission and began defending those who broke the law through their anti-war activities. They specialize in defending illegal aliens suspected of anti-American activity, and atheists who don't want Christians to mention the name of Christ or religion in the public arena. (Ironically, they think it's okay for Buddhists or Muslims to publicly recognize their gods!).

All of these groups are citizens and are protected by the Bill of Rights. But the ACLU is selective about whose rights it defends. They select some of the ten freedoms in the Bill of Rights and ignore others. They base their values on human reasoning instead of the godly principles evident in the Declaration of Independence.

The Declaration is the political, philosophical and moral foundation of the Constitution. It was written first to justify the 13 original colonies for breaking away from English tyranny. It laid out a view of government that maintained that God, in His orderly creation, gives inalienable rights to mankind, and among them is the right to self-rule.

The Constitution was written 11 years after independence was won. The immediate purpose of the Constitution was to unite the colonies as a nation, and provide for orderly self-rule of and between the colonies. Each colony was already an individual, sovereign state, but under the Constitution the 13 states united under one Federal head. Although God is not mentioned in the Constitution, it clearly rises from the Declaration of Independence.

Our Founding Fathers were well aware of non-theistic (denying the Creator) thinking in their day. The Declaration of Independence refers to God as the source of law when it states that all men are "endowed by their Creator with certain unalienable Rights." It goes on to say "That to secure these rights, Governments are instituted among Men."

We conclude then, that they made a conscious decision to endorse belief in a Creator, *intentionally distinguishing American government from other governments* of their day.

The America of our Fathers

The American form of government was thus instituted by the Founders who represented the people. The Constitution applied the values of the Declaration of Independence. The God-given right to self-rule was to be protected by a separation of powers. Three branches of government were created to keep a single branch from taking too much power.

Thomas Jefferson was concerned that the courts would go beyond their authority and, instead of interpreting the law, would begin making law. He knew this would create an oligarchy, the rule of a few over the many. The amendment process was created to accommodate any change that needed to come.

It is popular today for some to say in ignorance that America was *not* founded as a Christian nation. Here are some historical facts that contradict those assumptions, and summarize and document our Founders' belief and trust in God.

On May 16, 1776, the Continental Congress appointed an official national day of fasting and prayer for the colonies. It read:

> The Congress . . . desirous . . . to have people of all ranks and degrees duly impressed with a solemn sense of God's superintending providence, and of their duty, devoutly to rely . . . on His aid and direction . . . Do earnestly recommend Friday, the 17th day of May be observed by the colonies as a day of humiliation, fasting, and prayer; that we may, with united hearts, confess and bewailed our manifold sins and transgressions, and, by sincere repentance and amendment of life, appease God's righteous displeasure, and, through the merits and mediation of Jesus Christ, obtain this pardon and forgiveness.

A year later, on September 11, 1777, Congress ordered the importation of 20,000 Bibles for the American troops. The law read as follows:

> The use of the Bible is so universal and its importance so great that your committee refers the above to the consideration of Congress, and if Congress shall not think it expedient to order the importation of types and paper, the Committee recommends that Congress will order the Committee of Commerce to import 20,000 Bibles from Holland, Scotland, or

> elsewhere, into the different parts of the States of
> the Union.
>
> Whereupon it was resolved accordingly to direct said
> Committee of Commerce to import 20,000 copies of
> the Bible.

Congress even authorized its endorsement to be printed on the front page of the edition of the Bible approved for the American people:

> Whereupon, Resolved, that the Unites States in
> Congress assembled . . . recommend this edition of
> the Bible to the inhabitants of the Unites States,
> and hereby authorize [Robert Aitken] to publish this
> recommendation in the manner he shall think proper.

Calling it "An Ordinance for the Government of the Territory of the United States," a law was passed by the United States Congress and signed into law by President George Washington on August 4, 1789. It read:

> Article III: *Religion, morality, and knowledge being
> necessary to good government and the happiness
> of mankind, schools and the means of education
> shall be forever encouraged.*

Constitutional scholar Herbert Titus, a Harvard attorney and former ACLU attorney, says, "I used to be an ACLU cooperating attorney. In the 1960s there was a definite plan to rid this nation of all public displays of any religious symbol of this nation's founding."

An Enemy Betrays America

On January 10, 1963, Congressman Albert S. Herlong Jr., D-Fla., read into the *Congressional Record* a list of 45 goals the

Communist Party U.S.A. had adopted. I won't give them all, but here are a few of those goals that the ACLU is currently using in its quest to destroy America's culture and traditions:

~ Use technical decisions of the courts to weaken basic American institutions by claiming their activities violate civil rights.

~ Get control of the schools. Use them as transmission belts for socialism and current communist propaganda. Soften the curriculum. Get control of teachers associations. Put the party line in textbooks.

~ Continue discrediting American culture by degrading all form of artistic expression.

~ Eliminate all laws governing obscenity by calling them "censorship" and a violation of free speech and free press.

~ Break down cultural standards of morality by promoting pornography and obscenity in books, magazines, motion pictures, radio and television.

~ Present homosexuality, degeneracy and promiscuity as "normal, natural and healthy."

~ Infiltrate the churches and replace revealed religion with "social" religion. Discredit the Bible and emphasize the need for intellectual maturity that does not need a religious crutch.

~ Eliminate prayer or any form of religious expression in the schools on the grounds that it violates the principle of separation of church and state.

~ Belittle all forms of American culture and discourage the teaching of American history on the ground that it was only a minor part of the big picture.

~ Discredit the family as an institution. Encourage promiscuity and easy divorce.

This chipping away of America's freedoms from within our own country is having devastating results. For example, the ACLU is not only a leading advocate of same-sex "marriage," but has publicly expressed support for polygamy and polyamory (so-called "open" marriage) as well. The ACLU Policy Guide reads:

> *The ACLU believes that criminal and civil laws prohibiting or penalizing the practice of plural marriage [polygamy or polyamory] violate constitutional protections of freedom of expression and association, freedom of religion, and privacy for personal relationships among consenting adults.*

While many accept the ACLU as a mainstream organization, their history tells a drastically different story.

Money and Control

What the ACLU is really after, however, is money and control. They want your money and they want to control you. They have learned to manipulate the court system so that they are often able to persuade a liberal judge to give *them* money to finance their lawsuits. Just follow the money.

When you hear from the ACLU, they are filing a lawsuit against some value of our Judeo-Christian heritage. When they win, they then sue for legal fees. Alan Sears of the Alliance Defense Fund, said, "It's ridiculous what the ACLU has done to the people of this country, especially small school district officials, with their campaign of fear, intimidation and disinformation."

~ After the ACLU won a suit overturning an amendment to the Nebraska Constitution defining marriage as the union of one man and one woman—an amendment approved, by the way, by 70 percent of Nebraska voters—the ACLU was awarded $156,960.

~   The ACLU sued the Boy Scouts of America, and San Diego had to nullify a lease it had signed with them because the Boy Scouts requires kids to promise to live a "morally straight" life. The federal judge awarded the ACLU $790,000.

~   The ACLU sued Barrow County, Georgia, to remove a display of the Ten Commandments from the courthouse. Taxpayers had to pay $150,000 *and* remove the display.

~   The Florida Supreme Court established the Florida Bar Foundation which then paid the ACLU of Florida $615,500 from 1990 to 1997.

~   The ACLU was awarded $121,500 after suing to remove a monument outside of the Kentucky Capitol building.

~   In 2001, the ACLU was awarded nearly $300,000 after suing to overturn abortion regulations in Kentucky. They were given a similar amount in 1994.

~   A Tennessee county was forced to pay the ACLU $50,000 after losing a legal battle to preserve a display of the Ten Commandments.

~   After winning a lawsuit to prevent Loudoun County, Virginia, from installing pornography filters on public library computers, the ACLU was awarded $37,037.

~   Taxpayers were forced to pay ACLU lawyers a whopping $63,000 after they sued to remove a World War I Memorial Cross from the Mojave National Preserve.

~   After suing to remove a Ten Commandments display from the Habersham County, Georgia, courthouse, the ACLU received $74,462 from Georgia taxpayers.

~ The ACLU was awarded $25,000 after suing an Arkansas county for telling the child's parents that the 14-year-old boy was living an openly gay lifestyle in school.

~ Cobb County, Georgia, had a seven-word sticker on the district's biology books. The stickers read, "Evolution is a theory, not a fact." When the ACLU successfully sued to have them removed, Cobb County taxpayers had to give the ACLU $135,000.

~ When the ACLU sued Pasco, Washington because city fathers wanted to remove a picture of a naked woman from the City Hall, the city of Pasco was forced to pay the ACLU $75,000.

~ The residents of Seattle, Washington, were ordered to pay $52,000 to the ACLU for defending a student's "right" to mock the assistant principal in sexual online parodies.

~ Multnomah County taxpayers in Oregon had to pay the ACLU a whopping $110,000 after the ACLU sued them for allowing the Boy Scouts of America to recruit on public school campuses.

~ Operation Rescue had to pay the ACLU $111,000 after a lawsuit in which the ACLU sought to prevent the organization from picketing near abortion clinics.

~ After the Supreme Court declared the Nebraska partial birth abortion ban unconstitutional, the ACLU reaped a $6,000,000 bonanza from this and similar lawsuits in 30 states.

~ In 1954, the citizens of San Diego, California, erected the Mount Soledad War Memorial to honor the veterans of the Korean War. Because the memorial incorporated a cross, the ACLU and a local atheist named Philip Paulson filed a lawsuit in 1989, challenging its presence on city land. When 76 percent of the voters in San Diego County approved an initiative to transfer the property in order to preserve the memorial, the

ACLU objected again; and in 2002, the Ninth Circuit Court of Appeals, called the most liberal in the country, ruled the transfer of the property unconstitutional because it "guaranteed the preservation of the cross." The ACLU was awarded $230,000, because it brought the suit!

Attacking America from Within

While seeking to ban God from the public arena, the ACLU supports the right to unlimited access to pornography on public school computers. It is actively fighting Internet filtering laws.

While supporting a recent Massachusetts law legalizing same-sex marriage, the ACLU wants the U.S. Supreme Court to force all states in the Union to follow suit. Yet, the Bill of Rights (that the ACLU says it defends) protects states' rights to make their own laws!

On the Internet once could be foundwhat was called the ACLU Policy Issues Statement. At this writing, it has been withdrawn and the organization will allow only selected persons to see it, although it is a nonprofit organization. Here are some of its policies:

~ Policy 211 called for the legalization of prostitution.

~ Policy 4 called for defending all pornography, including child porn, as free speech.

~ Policy 210 called for the decriminalization and legalization of all drugs.

~ Policy 264 called for the promotion of homosexuality.

~ Policy 18 opposed music and movie ratings.

~ Policy 262 opposed requiring minors seeking an abortion to notify their parents. It also opposed requiring laws notifying a spouse in cases of abortion.

ACLU policies also call for defending or promoting euthanasia, polygamy, government control of church institutions, gun control, tax-funded abortion, and many other things that affect our everyday lives. (See policies 47, 85, 91, 133, 261, 263, 271, 402.)

On Guard Against All Enemies

The tallest structure in Washington, D.C. is the Washington Monument. By law, nothing can be built taller than the Washington Monument. Do you know what is inscribed at the pinnacle of the Washington Monument, the tallest structure in our nation's capitol? These words from Scripture: "Let God be praised."

Christians in America must stand for the right and be ever vigilant in the defense of freedom. Our forefathers had divergent religious views, but they did not forbid or ban religious expression or practice. We have precedent, however, in more recent times. Consider this.

In *McIntosh vs. U.S.* (1930), the Supreme Court ruled:

> *We are a Christian people, according to our motto. The right of religious freedom demands acknowledgment with reverence and the duty of obedience to the will of God.*

In *Zorach vs. Clauson* (1952), the Supreme Court concluded:

> *We are a religious people whose institutions presuppose a Supreme Being. We guarantee the freedom to worship as one chooses. We make room*

for as wide a variety of beliefs and creeds as the spiritual needs of man deem necessary. We sponsor an attitude on the part of government that shows no partiality to any one group and that lets each flourish according to the zeal of its adherents and the appeal of its dogma.

In 1954, Chief Justice Earl Warren said:

I believe that no one can read the history of our country without realizing that the Good Book and the Spirit of the Savior have from the beginning been our guiding geniuses (Time, *Feb 15, 1954*).

The Bible said in Proverbs 14:34, "Righteousness exalts a nation." Psalm 33:12 says, "Blessed is the nation whose God is the Lord, the people He chose for His inheritance."

French writer Alexis de Tocqueville, visited America in 1831, and wrote the following:

I sought for the greatness of the United States in her commodious harbors, her ample rivers, her fertile fields, and boundless forests—and it was not there. I sought for it in her rich mines, her vast world commerce, her public school system, and in her institutions of higher learning—and it was not there. I looked for it in her democratic Congress and her matchless Constitution—and it was not there.

Not until I went into the churches of America and heard her pulpits flame with righteousness *did I understand the secret of her genius and power. America is great because America is good, and if America ever ceases to be good, America will cease to be great!*

I believe the United States of America is a nation of prophecy, chosen by God to be a vineyard nation. In keeping His vineyard, we must acknowledge that God raised us up to be a righteous nation and to preach His gospel to all the world. We must forever be on guard against the enemies from within and from without.

Clearly, America can be found in prophecy when we compare the spiritual patterns of ancient Israel and the governmental patterns of Rome to our history and to our democracy. Will we fall into unbelief as ancient Israel and into moral decay as ancient Rome? Will such organizations as the ACLU and their fellow travelers become the voice of secular America while Christians and religious Jews become their targets for spiritual assassination?

Only if the righteous stand up, speak up and intercede for our nation can God's hand intervene on our behalf. If Christians do not stand up for our spiritual heritage and defend our rights to preach, teach and proclaim the gospel, we may find such groups as the ACLU and their fellow travelers have secularized Christianity out of America.

If the patterns of ancient Israel and the Roman Empire correlate with the prophetic history and destiny of America, then we must discover where they failed and not let it happen to us. Israel's sin was spiritual unbelief.

The Roman Empire was tolerant until they believed in every god, and there was no absolute truth. Immorality seized the empire and choked it into oblivion.

It is time for the church to intercede as Abraham did for his nephew, Lot, so that we can keep our families from the future judgments that are to come. History is a teacher and we are its students. May we learn well lest we repeat the failures of past empires.

Bibliography

Book of Jasher. Muscogee, Oklahoma: Artisan. 1988.

E. Raymond Capt. *The Stone Kingdom, America*. Muskogee, Oklahoma: Artisan. 2004.

Timothy Crater and Ranelda Hunsicker. *In God We Trust: Stories of Faith in American History*. Colorado Springs: ChariotVictor. 1997.

Richard Kelly Hoskins. *War Cycles/Peace Cycles*. Lynchburg, Virginia: Virginia Publishing. 2000.

Alexander Roberts and James Donaldson, Eds. *The Ante-Nicene Fathers, v. VII*. Grand Rapids: Wm. B. Eerdmans. 1989.

W.E. Vine. *A Comprehensive Dictionary of the Originial Greek Words with their Precise Meanings for English Readers*. Peabody, Massachusetts: Hendrickson. N.D.

William Whiston, Tr. *Complete Works of Flavius Josephus*. Grand Rapids: Kregel. 1960, 1978.

http://www.aclu.org

http://www.reclaimamerica.org

DIAGRAMS & ILLUSTRATIONS

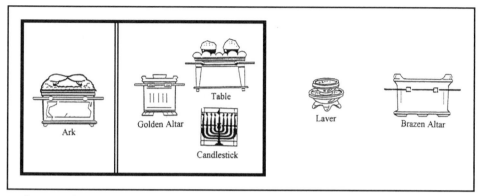

A diagram showing the rectangular shape of Moses' tabernacle. This also shows the position of the holy furniture in the Wilderness Tabernacle.

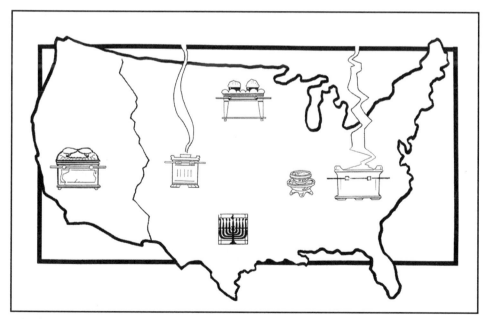

The furniture of the tabernacle overlaid onto a map of the continental United States of America. The position of the holy furniture and the corresponding regions within the U.S. suggest that our nation was uniquely and divinely established by the God of Israel. The U.S. seems to be God's modern-day wilderness tabernacle.

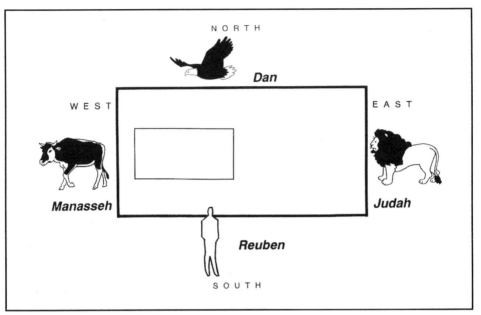

This drawing shows the positions and emblems of the four main tribes of ancient Israel.

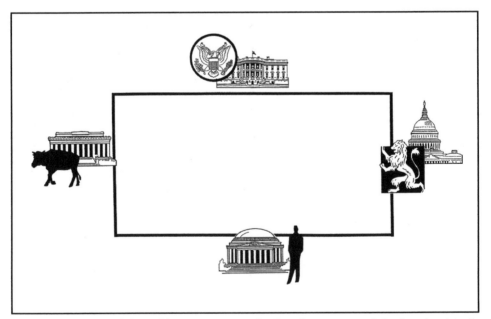

The tribe emblems of the wilderness camp can be found in or around the four landmarks bordering the National Mall. The Capitol Building has a lion, the Jefferson Memorial has a man, the Lincoln Memorial has a connection to an ox and the White House is home to the President, on whose emblem is the eagle.